HEKE-NUKU-MAI-NGA-IWI

BUSBY

HEKE-NUKU-MAI-NGA-IWI

BUSBY

NOT HERE BY CHANCE

JEFF EVANS

HUIA

First published in 2015 by Huia Publishers
39 Pipitea Street, PO Box 12280
Wellington, Aotearoa New Zealand
www.huia.co.nz

ISBN 978-1-77550-169-5

A catalogue record for this book is available from the National Library of New Zealand

Published with the assistance of

creative nz
ARTS COUNCIL OF NEW ZEALAND TOI AOTEAROA

CONTENTS

ACKNOWLEDGEMENTS: HEC BUSBY

In a book such as this, the first thing to say is that although there are some very important people who helped, there is no one person who can be identified as having made the greatest contribution to its completion. To mention individuals by name would, I am sure, offend people who feel that in either a direct or an indirect way they have helped me. That is not the intention of this book, which I see as a book by everyone for everyone.

More importantly, however, this book has been written on the basis that while we can do things as individuals, we are representatives of the many generations that have preceded us and the many generations that will follow us. In other words, this book has been written on a very simple but very Māori principle: that of 'Te tangata kotahi, ki tana rau kotahi' – An individual does not stand alone but represents the many generations that have passed on.

That said, there are a lot of individuals to whom I am most grateful for helping me to achieve what I have. They have been mentioned throughout this book, and their contributions, either individually or collectively, have resulted in the taonga and koha that I have received becoming available to the present and all future generations.

Although what I have left will benefit Māori in particular, Māori are but one of many seafaring peoples of the Pacific Ocean. The contributions of our Pacific whanaunga, especially that of Mau Piailug from Satawal in Micronesia and Nainoa Thompson and Clay Bertelmann, both from Hawai'i, have been the catalyst that enabled me to fulfil the waka dreams and aspirations of some of our kaumātua. It is for this reason that I have referred to Mau, specifically, as the 'missing link' in this revival of a great tradition.

Nā Hec Busby

INTRODUCTION

On 22 October 1992 the double-hulled canoe Te Aurere sailed through Ngātangi'ia Pass into Avana Harbour. Her arrival signalled the completion of a twenty-one-day storm-ravaged voyage, and marked her as the first voyaging canoe to arrive in Rarotonga directly from New Zealand in perhaps 600 years. The Māori Queen, Te Atairangikaahu, was there to witness the event, as was the Premier of the Cook Islands, Sir Geoffrey Henry. Media from across the Pacific had gathered to report on the historic homecoming, and an excited crowd, swollen by hundreds of performers and tourists on the island for the Festival of Pacific Arts, lined the shoreline.

The voyage, envisioned and planned by the then sixty-year-old Hec Busby, had followed in the wake of Tūmoana, an ancestor who had sailed to Aotearoa sometime between 1100 and 1300AD aboard the canoe Tinana[1] and later returned to his Pacific homeland. The catalyst for Te Aurere's voyage, however, had come in the form of an athletic twenty-nine-year-old Hawaiian who visited Hec in late 1983. Nainoa Thompson was preparing to guide the voyaging canoe Hōkūle'a into the central Pacific and was also considering voyaging to Aotearoa, but before he would commit he wanted to establish a relationship with both the tangata whenua and the land itself. His initial two-week-long stay with Hec would go a long way towards cementing those relationships.

Thompson's visit would have consequences far beyond his own needs, however. His presence in Aotearoa would ultimately inspire the revival of blue-water voyaging among his hosts. Hec, fascinated by the possibility of seeing a voyaging canoe sailing once again in the coastal waters of Northland, became captivated with the idea of building a waka hourua of his own. It was an ambitious goal for a man who was yet to build his first waka, but Hec had the confidence to dream big and the resolve to see his dreams realised. His resulting journey into the world of voyaging would result in both a spiritual awakening and a metaphysical passage that would see him stand among his ancestors, invoking their knowledge and support to reinvigorate their feats.

The canoe's true genesis came from the period of pre-Māori history when the ancestors of the Māori first began migrating to Aotearoa. It was a period of heroic deeds by men and women whose names would be remembered through traditions, whakataukī and waiata. Many of their stories have remained at the forefront of Māori consciousness to this day. Indeed, it was the stories of these seafaring ancestors that had captivated Hec's imagination as a child and, undoubtedly, cultivated his lifelong love of waka and waka culture.

Hec's more recent forebears are of course equally important when it comes to understanding the man he would become.

With rangatira of note lining his whakapapa, it's no great surprise that he excelled wherever he focused his energy – especially after being singled out for mentoring by his elders once he had proven himself.

The signs of his promise were evident early on. It was as a young man that he had first shown a tireless capacity for hard, physical work and displayed a dogged determination to see undertakings through to their conclusions: traits that he would later rely upon when, still in his mid-twenties, he started his own bridge-building business. It was no surprise to those who knew him that the business grew steadily and eventually flourished.

In time his commercial experience and street smarts would make Hec a highly regarded member of several tribal committees, and would result in his appointment to a number of prestigious roles, including being named the first kaitiaki for the waka taua Ngātokimatawhaorua after her relaunch in 1974, as well as being asked to take his place on the paepae at Waitangi: two roles that would accelerate his personal growth and eventually lead to opportunities for mentoring by kaumātua from outside Hec's tribal boundaries.

Hec was content to lend a hand wherever he could, be it by helping around the committee table or by offering vehicles and supplies for working bees. However, a growing sense of urgency to safeguard the remaining strands of traditional mātauranga surfaced during the late 1960s and early 1970s, leading to perhaps Hec's most important contribution for his people: a willingness to act as both a repository and a guardian of cultural knowledge. In time his role would lead to him becoming a critical figure in the renaissance of a number of arts in the Far North – arts as diverse as whakairo, mau rākau, kapa haka, karakia tawhito and of course waka construction and use. In his later years, Hec's role would change significantly, but still draw on the knowledge he had accumulated when he began to represent Te Rarawa in Treaty of Waitangi claims and various other forums.

Despite his influence across several forms, for most New Zealanders Hec is perhaps best known for the voyages of his waka Te Aurere, the vessel inspired by Thompson's 1983 visit. Recognised throughout the Pacific as one of the pre-eminent contemporary voyaging canoes, her very existence and ongoing success can be largely attributed to a combination of Hec's determination and Thompson's mentoring. A devotee and student of the famed master navigator Mau Piailug, Thompson was also the conduit to the Carolinian's navigational knowledge for Hec, presenting him with the last piece of the jigsaw to complete his own voyaging puzzle. It has been far from a one-way learning environment though, as Nainoa often acknowledges. The Hawaiian considers Hec his own mentor when it comes to connecting to the ancestors and their ways.

I first met Hec in 1999, seven years after Te Aurere's epic voyage to Rarotonga. I had travelled to the Bay of Islands to take in events on Waitangi Day, and after striking up a conversation with Stanley Conrad I was introduced to the man himself. Of course I knew of him. He was already well on his way to iconic status within waka circles, and I remember being struck by his commanding presence: he was clearly the boss when it came to anything waka related, and no one, as far as I can recall, as much as hinted at questioning a single one of his decisions. Ours was by necessity a brief meeting – he had several waka and their crews to organise – but it was there that I first had an inkling that I might one day write his biography, encouraged as I was by his openness and willingness to take the time to talk on the day. I've no idea why the thought occurred to me. I had never written anything as challenging as a biography, and what's more I was clearly an outsider; my tenuous connection to his world was by way of a pair of modest publications I had written on waka, and I was sure he'd not heard of me, although there did seem to be a connection of sorts between us.

As it happened he was interested in having his story told, and in fact in the past one or two other writers had started on his biography only to abandon their work, perhaps defeated by the relative remoteness of their subject's home. Unsurprisingly he was a little guarded when I finally broached the subject some months later. Instead of the hoped-for positive reply, I was offered a place on Te Aurere for an overnight sail from Auckland to Waitangi.

I presumed it was a test of sorts, and if so, it was one I failed. I did, however, manage to distinguish myself twice during the short voyage north; firstly by running off a pod of dolphins with some flash photography at dusk, and then by throwing up my breakfast the following morning. To say it was an inauspicious start to our relationship is an understatement.

And yet, eventually, he agreed to the project, although – perhaps due to my performance on his beloved waka – it would be another eighteen months before we would start in earnest.

Progress wasn't without its challenges, however. Countless trips north and dozens of interviews transcribed between late 2001 and 2004 were followed by a long break in proceedings, and it wasn't until 2008 that the project gathered further momentum with a series of face-to-face and phone interviews with Hec and his family and friends – but finally we are here.

I owe a great deal to Stanley Conrad, Jack Thatcher, Martin Bercic and Nainoa Thompson, who each spent many hours recalling the experiences they have shared with Hec. Their input has helped to bring this book to life. Had it not been for their contributions, the book would have undoubtedly been the poorer. I would like to thank Walter Busby and acknowledge the late Hector Morris Busby for sharing precious family memories from their youth, and also Hec's stepdaughter Gina Harding and her husband Michael, who ensured Hec and I had comfortable surroundings and sufficient cups of tea to see us through numerous mammoth interview sessions at Hec's Doubtless Bay home. Special thanks are due to Sir Don McKinnon, Haare Williams, Karl Johnstone, Ben Finney, Sam Low, Joe O'Connor and Haami Piripi, who were all generous with their time and memories at critical times along the way, as were Robert Gable and Pita Paraone, who helped me far more than their brief appearances in the book suggest.

Thanks to Patu Hohepa, Judy Huntsman, Claire Murdoch, Tumarangai Sciascia and Peter Dowling, who all provided support when asked. I am also grateful to the Te Ahu Heritage archivist Lynda Hammond, who made me aware of several early and important newspaper clippings related to the Busby family. I would also like to acknowledge Creative New Zealand, which provided funding that allowed me to take time off work to concentrate on finishing the manuscript, and the Auckland War Memorial Museum, which allowed me an extended leave of absence to get the book across the line.

Of course no book exists without a publisher who believes in the author and subject; the team at Huia Publishers has provided wonderful support throughout the project. Their foresight, experience and understanding have made it a pleasure to work with them.

Much of this book is based on Hec's own memories of events; wherever possible those memories have been checked against newspaper reports or corroborated by family and friends. That Hec's recall of various events occasionally differs from that of others shouldn't be a surprise. We each have our own perspectives and our own focus, and in recalling his long and full life, Hec – at least in this regard – is no different to the rest of us.

Jeff Evans, 2015

Notes

[1] Waitangi Tribunal. *Muriwhenua Fishing Report* (Wai 22, 1988), p. 247.

1

TŪPUNA

Heke-nuku-mai-nga-iwi (Hec) Busby, son of Timoti Iehu and Winifred Ruth Busby, was born in the family homestead on 1 August 1932. Overseeing the birth were the child's grandmother Raiha (Eliza) Piripi and another relative, Heeni Pita. The two women, both experienced midwives, were responsible for looking after all the pregnancies in Pukepoto and the surrounding area, and, as expected, there were no complications with the infant's birth. In later years Raiha would tell the child that the honour of naming him had fallen to his great-aunt Rehu (Whenu) Rewhiti. No explanation remains for her choice of name, but in time it would prove prophetic.

The homestead, situated between Kaitāia and Ahipara and perched on one of a series of low hills above Pukepoto settlement, overlooked a ribbon of land that stretched several kilometres out to the moody Tasman Sea. The fertile soil of the flats below the house was part of a large tract of tribal territory that swept from the upper shores of the Hokianga Harbour to Kaitāia in the north and across to Mangōnui in the east, and it had sustained Te Rarawa ever since they had first established their mana whenua over the territory hundreds of years earlier.

Hec's ancestors on his Māori side were respected chiefs with links back to a number of migration canoes, including the Māmari, Tākitimu, Ngātokimatawhaorua and Tinana. Noted among his more immediate ancestors are the great fighting chief Tarutaru, an important ancestor to a number of northern iwi, and Pōroa, a grandson of Tarutaru and a high-ranking chief of Te Rarawa in his own right. At his peak Pōroa was recognised as the rangatira over the land from Kaitāia to Ahipara, and it is remembered that during times of conflict he was able to rely on the support of the strong Ngāpuhi chief Hongi Hika.

The fighting prowess of the family didn't necessarily stop there. It is quite likely that Hec's great-great-grandfather, Te Maru Te Ripi (later known as Puhipi Te Ripi or simply Puhipi),[1] was an active participant during inter-tribal fighting under Pōroa. Indeed, he was probably in the thick of the action as a young warrior during Te Rarawa's last major battle with the neighbouring Te Aupōuri tribe, around 1824. The battle, named Te Oneroa, was a violent struggle that Te Rarawa eventually won, thanks in no small part to the assistance of Hongi Hika's warriors. It was at the conclusion of this battle that Pōroa famously drew a line in the sand of Te Oneroa-a-Tōhē (Ninety Mile Beach) with his taiaha to mark the boundary between Te Aupōuri and Te Rarawa. Several marriages between rangatira of the two tribes were then proposed. Such marriages, termed hohou te rongo – binding together in peace – were commonly resorted to in the hope that they would cement an end to hostilities. Among those married was

Te Ripi, Pōroa's nephew through his sister Te Ruakuru, who took Meri Ngaroto, a high-born Te Aupōuri woman, as his wife.

Regrettably their union was never blessed with a child to carry Te Ripi's chiefly bloodlines, and as was the custom of the time, Te Ripi eventually took a second wife, Akinihi,[2] with whom he had Hec's great-grandfather Timoti Wharemate Puhipi.

The middle decades of the nineteenth century were uncertain times for Māori, and a particularly challenging period for their chiefs. Not only were Māori still involved in inter-tribal conflict, but the influx of Pākehā into the country was accelerating from a trickle to a deluge. The Te Rarawa position, determined under paramount chief Nōpera (Noble) Panakareao, was to encourage Pākehā to settle in their territory, primarily for trade purposes, but also so his people could learn from them. Panakareao also invited missionaries to settle among Te Rarawa, pledging them both land and protection. These missionaries would eventually become trusted intermediaries between Māori and Pākehā, and their influence among Māori grew to substantial levels over time. Indeed, by early 1840 most of the principal Te Rarawa chiefs had been persuaded to align with the European churches. Te Ripi was baptised into the Anglican faith on 15 January 1840, taking the name Puhipi (a transliteration of Busby – James Busby, the official British Resident, being his baptismal sponsor). The baptism was performed by Reverend Richard Taylor and duly recorded in the register of baptisms in the parish of Kaitāia. Te Ripi was described as an 'adult chief', and his abode noted as 'Pukepoto'. From that time forward he used the name Puhipi, which was then passed down through his only son Timoti Wharemate, who took Puhipi as his surname.

The year of Puhipi's baptism was of course a significant year in the wider context of New Zealand history. The signing of the Treaty of Waitangi in the Bay of Islands was followed by a series of hui in other parts of the country where chiefs were invited to debate the worth of the Treaty and decide whether to go into partnership with the British Crown. At the end of April, nearly three months after the initial signing at Waitangi, Nōpera Panakareao hosted such a hui. Prominent among those who spoke was Puhipi, who said: 'Before the Pākehā came we loved our own people. We sometimes quarrelled and then made war; then we made peace again and rubbed noses; then we had another battle. I am glad you are come; let our hearts be one.'[3] Puhipi, perhaps already swayed by Panakareao, was in favour of formalising the partnership, but still went on to question how the British, who would be based in the Bay of Islands, proposed to settle disputes in the Far North when they would be so far away. Other chiefs stood and spoke, until Panakareao, asserting his right as paramount chief, delivered the final speech. Comfortable with the translation of the Treaty and the explanation of unfamiliar words that he had received from the missionary William Gilbert Puckey the previous day, Panakareao was firmly in favour of the Treaty. The future, he insisted, lay in having Pākehā dwell among them.[4] With Panakareao's decision to support the Treaty accepted as the final word on the matter, the assembled chiefs duly signed the Treaty, and the hui concluded with a stirring haka and a 'general discharge of musketry'.[5] As was the Māori custom of the period, the celebratory feast that followed was provided entirely at Panakareao's expense.

Puhipi lived for another thirty-two years, dying, coincidently, on the anniversary of the initial signing of the Treaty of Waitangi. His passing and tangi were recorded by Henry Matthew Stowell, a frequent contributor to newspapers and journals who wrote under the pen name Hare Hongi:

> It was at 10 o'clock in the evening of the 6th of February 1872, that Te Puhipi died at his home. Pukepoto, which lies between Kaitaia and Ahipara (the Ninety Mile Beach). Although quite an aged man his end came on so gradually that it occupied some three weeks.
>
> Being a high chief of the great Rarawa tribe, there was a great gathering of the tribal members and their representative high chiefs ... All were gathered from Hokianga, Whangape, Herekino, Ahipara, Kaitaia, Awanui, Kareponia, Pamapuria, and even further parts.
>
> Having dined, the 'ngarahu' (war dance) of the Rarawa was performed; in that some 600 took part. Invigorating! Yes. Provisions there were in plenty. And although the mourners remained a whole week – Puhipi was buried on the 10th – those were not consumed.[6]

With most if not all senior Te Rarawa chiefs attending the tangi, the opportunity was taken to discuss a successor to Puhipi, and at the conclusion of the deliberation Timoti Wharemate Puhipi, the deceased's only son, was chosen to lead his people. It would prove to be an inspired choice.

Born about 1834 and baptised some ten years later, Timoti received a very good education by the standards of rural New Zealand at the time. After completing school he was appointed a lay reader in the Anglican Church, and would conduct services at his kāinga for many years. Later, while in his mid-thirties, he attended the 1870 Anglican Synod in Auckland, where he and two others represented the people of Pukepoto. In between times he also studied to become a mission-trained teacher under the careful supervision of Church Missionary Society missionary Reverend Joseph Matthews.

When Timoti inherited his father's position, he took on the responsibility of overseeing the general well-being of his people. It was a role he would relish. One of his first objectives was to solicit the establishment of a Native School at Ahipara. Within weeks of his father's passing, Timoti had written to the Government offering to build a church that would double as a school building, as well as pledging to contribute towards the teacher's salary. The Government, he continued, would need only to meet the balance of the teacher's salary and provide a home for the teacher, for which the tribe would give them the land. Unsurprisingly, given the generous terms on offer, the arrangement was agreed upon in quick order and the school duly opened.

Timoti also expended energy negotiating with the Crown to make land available for settlement, and great hope was held out that a new wave of settlers would make their homes in Te Rarawa territory after a visit from Land Purchase Commissioner

Lieutenant-Colonel Thomas McDonnell in 1873. The desired surge in settlers failed to eventuate, however – at least in the numbers Puhipi envisioned – and rather than being remembered as the beginning of a prosperous chapter in Te Rarawa history, the period would instead be remembered for a typhoid outbreak that devastated the population in and around Ahipara in 1874. Among the three dozen or so souls claimed by the disease was Timoti's wife Marara. Her death and the generally desperate state of affairs in Ahipara and the surrounding lands at the time were reported by Native Land Purchase Agent E T Brissenden to the Native Minister:

> While at Ahipara I had occasion to see Timoti Puhipi and his people, and found them in a most deplorable state. They were suffering from typhoid fever; thirty-four of their number had died within three weeks. Timoti Puhipi had lost his wife and was seriously ill, as were many others when I left them (7th July). They were dark and dissatisfied at the neglect of the Government officer of their district, saying he had not been near them, nor offered them the slightest assistance in the time of their great trouble. I took the liberty of providing them with a few necessary comforts, and gave them 25 pounds in cash on Government account, which I hope will meet with your approval.[7]

Marara left behind a grieving husband and three children: two sons, Riapo (Leopold) and Poroa, and a daughter, Heeni.

Timoti didn't stay unmarried for long, however. It was accepted that a chief of his standing should have the support of a wife in both public and private life, and his wedding to Maata (Martha) Murray, the daughter of Scottish shipwright John Murray and Kataraina Te Koni (Te Rarawa, Te Aupōuri and Ngāti Kurī), occurred a mere ten months after Marara's death. If he had hoped for an understated wedding, it wasn't to be. W Tangata, a minister with the Gospel of Christ, reported on the occasion for the national newspaper *Te Waka Maori* on 27 April:

> Pukepoto, Kaitaia, 14th April, 1875.
>
> On the 7th of April instant, Timoti Puhipi Te Ripi and his wife Martha were married. (Timoti is an Assessor of the Queen, and a descendant of Pooroa.) At 8 o'clock in the morning they were escorted by one hundred of the tribe to Kaitaia, for the purpose of having the ceremony performed at that place. Mary Ann and a number of other young girls were then chosen as bridesmaids to accompany them to the church. The bride and bridegroom were arrayed in garments suitable for the occasion, and were married by the Rev. J. Matthews.
>
> After the ceremony was concluded, they returned to Pukepoto. As they approached the settlement they were put forward in front of the procession which escorted them, one bearing the Queen's flag marching by their side. The main body of the people were formed in column at the village awaiting their arrival, while the women waved them onward with cries of welcome. Then the escort of one hundred, all mounted on horseback, who conducted the married couple, halted for the space of about two minutes, whilst the column at the village sang with one accord a

> song of welcome. At the conclusion they were conducted to a house set apart for their use.

Timoti's bride was one of a growing number of offspring from marriages between European migrants – mostly British – and high-ranking Māori mothers.[8] Maata's father, Alfred John Murray (known as John), had been born John Borrowdale on 3 January 1813 in Moffat, Scotland, and had arrived in New Zealand as a twenty-four-year-old in 1837. His arrival coincided with a period when it was common for Pākehā males living away from the relative safety of settler townships to marry local women of high birth. As English traveller Edward Markham wrote in his book *New Zealand or Recollections of it*:

> [I]t is not safe to live in the Country without a Chief's daughter as a protection as they are always backed by their tribe and you are not robbed or molested in that case; they become useful and very much attached if used well and will suffer incredible persecution for the men they live with. But for now it may be noted that both sides saw intermarriage as commercially advantageous: to the trader, to secure the goods; and to Māori, to secure the trader. In any event, those who married into the community had a measure of protection.[9]

Although such marriages may have been actively encouraged under most circumstances, Kataraina Te Koni's budding relationship with Murray was, at least initially, opposed by her family – a fact confirmed in a family story from the period, as Hec recalls: 'Kataraina's people didn't want her to marry Murray, and at one point when her family suspected he was in the house with her, they came over to chase him out. Fortunately she saw them coming and hid him in one of those big old barrels that they used to store salted meat in. Well they didn't find him, and when she rushed over to let him out after they had left she found him half-suffocated and coughing like hell.' The story continued, perhaps mischievously, that this was how Murray got his Māori name Mare, which is both a transliteration of Murray and the Māori word for 'cough'. 'So he became known as Hone Mare.'

Soon after arriving in the Hokianga, Murray established what would in time become a successful boat-building business. Under Murray's auspices the *Elizabeth* was completed at Hokianga in 1851; the *Kataraina Borrowdale* was launched at Ahipara in 1868; and the *Halfcaste* (1881) and the *Te Rarawa* (1885) were both built at Boat Harbour, Tairua, on the Coromandel. Murray's boats had a reputation for fine lines and impressive speed through the water; especially the *Halfcaste*, which featured prominently in a story entitled 'Illicit Milkrun' recorded in the Murray family history, *The Beginning of a New Zealand Dynasty*:

> In 1881, a small 44ft cutter was built at Tairua by Alfred [John] Murray. She was named Halfcaste, and in 1883 was registered under the ownership of Hugh Anderson. In her short career, she earned a reputation for speed; but how much her speed was due to her design, and how much to the drive and motivation of her crew, we can only

> guess. According to Jack Petley, she enjoyed a 'roaring trade' distributing the produce of an illicit whiskey still at Boat Harbour.
>
> Her 'milk delivery' extended from Port Charles to Opotiki, and although she was often chased by revenue men, she was overtaken only once – by the revenue cutter Hawk. When the Hawk appeared, Halfcaste carefully dumped her precious consignment in the ocean, with a line and float attached, so that, after being declared clean, and the Hawk having disappeared, she was able to recover her cargo, and continue on her 'milk round'.[10]

Within a year of Timoti Wharemate Puhipi's marriage to Maata he had put his name forward as a candidate for the Northern Māori electoral seat. At age forty-two, he had already fashioned a fine record working tirelessly for his people and had proven himself an extremely capable leader both in their eyes and in the estimation of Pākehā. His defeat in the 1875–76 election therefore came as a surprise to many, including W B White, who had appointed Puhipi's father as a native assessor back in 1848. He observed:

> The natives of this district are naturally disappointed that Mr. Timoti Puhipi was only second on the list of candidates for the Northern District in the General Assembly. I thought there would have been a case of bribery at elections. It was stated the successful man was returned by the admission of the votes of little boys; but the fact was that some of Mr Puhipi's own people so much objected to his going from

the district, that they refrained from voting in numbers which, had they voted, would have placed him at the head of the poll.[11]

Timoti would go on to stand unsuccessfully for the Northern Māori seat in five elections before he finally gave up the dream of representing his people on the national stage. His lack of success did, however, allow him to continue his involvement in local issues, including the fight to have Pukepoto's school reopened. After it was closed in 1891, in part due to a decimated role after numerous families had left the settlement to work in the gum fields, Timoti sent a barrage of letters to the Government demanding either that it be reopened or that the land it stood upon, which he had provided, be formally returned. Perhaps unsurprisingly, the school was reopened.

Timoti continued advocating for the well-being of his people right up until his untimely death in September 1910; after being unwell for several months, he finally succumbed to a severe attack of bronchitis. An obituary published in the *North Auckland Age* soon after his death described him as 'a chief of great mana which was often exercised in quelling inter-tribal disputes, which were formerly of frequent occurrence'. The notice, published on 19 September, went on to report that a significant number of Europeans joined the large groups of Māori converging on Pukepoto to pay their last respects and that telegrams of sympathy had been received from the Bishop of Auckland, Māori parliamentarians Sir James Carroll and Sir Āpirana Ngata, and others.

Upon Timoti's death the chiefly line transferred to his eldest son from his first marriage, Riapo (Leopold) Busby. Riapo would go on to become a significant leader of Te Rarawa in the early years of the twentieth century, and he was responsible for organising one of the first memorials in the country to commemorate New Zealand's World War One dead. The monument, funded entirely through subscription, was unveiled in Kaitāia on 24 March 1916.

It was probably during the second decade of the twentieth century that the Puhipi family started to use the European version of their surname. No one recalls why the change was made, and it is possible that both names were used within the wider whānau for a number of years, but certainly by the mid-1930s 'Busby' seems to have been favoured.

Hec's own whakapapa comes through Riapo's younger half-brother Iehu Mumu Te Awha, (from Timoti Wharemate Puhipi's second marriage to Maata).[12] Mumu, or Mu as he was commonly known, was married to Raiha Piripi of Ngāti Kahu (who hailed from Doubtless Bay), and was recognised as a chief of some standing despite being from a second marriage. Unfortunately his rise to tribal prominence coincided with a period in which Māori social order was changing, and the overarching role of tribal chief was beginning to fade. Land, once communally owned and under the guardianship of rangatira, was being cut up into blocks and transferred into the names of individuals or small groups. Other areas where leaders had once had the final word, such as in matters of justice, were now firmly under the jurisdiction of the Crown.

Tribal chiefs did, however, retain authority on the marae, and it was here that a bitter confrontation caused a serious split among the families of Pukepoto in the 1920s, as Hec recalls: 'When Rātana came north to recruit followers in 1921 he stopped in at Taipā, but they weren't really interested in what he had to offer and they asked him to leave. When my grandfather Mu heard they had turned Rātana away, he drove his buggy over to Taipā to pick him up and take him to our marae at Pukepoto. I think he felt sorry for him being so far away from home and having been turned away by Ngāti Kahu. When they arrived back at Pukepoto, some of our people weren't very happy with my grandfather for bringing Rātana to the marae, but Mu just stood and told them, "It's my marae and he's my visitor. If you don't want to be involved in looking after him, leave!" Well, his stance caused a serious rift in the settlement, and those who left ended up building a second marae, which they called Te Rarawa. In the end Mu didn't convert to Rātana, but he was happy to hear the man out.'

Old before his time and with his health broken, Mu's final years were affected by drink, and he died in 1922 aged just forty-six, with a bottle of whisky beside his bed and his youngest child, Moira, not yet born. His death and subsequent tangi were reported on 24 April 1922 in the *Northland Age* under the headline 'A Large Gathering at Pukepoto':

> Jehu Timoti Puhipi died at his residence in Pukepoto, early on Sunday morning, at the age of 46. His death was not unexpected, and soon the people began to gather.

> The people for the different settlements generally arrived in parties, heralding their approach by calling out, according to old Maori custom – 'Haere, haere, haere atu kinga tupune.' ('Go, go, go, go, and join your forefathers!') From as far south as Hokianga, and north to Houhora they came, and soon one of the largest tangis this county has seen in some time was being held. On Sunday, the family flag, a present from the NZ Government, was flying at half-mast from Pukepoto Hall, where the tangi was being held. On Monday, the Southern Cross of the Te Patuu was on the flag pole, signifying that the sympathies of the Te Patuu's were with the Te Rarawas. Mu was a quiet and unassuming man, very popular with his people. His word was his bond, as he was wont to say.

Mu's death signalled the end of his immediate family's involvement in the highest level of Te Rarawa affairs for some decades. His son, Hec's father, Timoti Iehu Busby, was content representing his own family on their marae and concentrating most of his energies on running the family farm to support a large extended family. That alone was a big enough challenge for any man – let alone one yet to reach the age of twenty.

Notes

[1] And occasionally as Pohipi and Poihipi in government papers.

[2] Puckey, A. *Trading Cultures: A History of the Far North*, Wellington: Huia, 2011, p. 340.

[3] Buick, T L. *The Treaty of Waitangi: How New Zealand became a British Colony*. New Plymouth: Thomas Avery and Sons, 3rd edition, 1936, p. 184.

[4] Waitangi Tribunal. *Muriwhenua Fishing Report* (Wai 22, 1988), p. 40.

[5] Buick. *The Treaty of Waitangi*, p. 187.

[6] Henry Stowell (Hare Hongi). An Account of the Death of Puhipi Te Ripi. 1872, MS-Papers-0062-41, Alexander Turnbull Library, Wellington.

[7] Mr Brissenden to Hon. The Native Minister. 27 July 1874, *Appendices to the Journal of the House of Representatives*, 1875, G-7, pp. 15–16.

[8] Hone Te Koni (Te Aupōuri, Te Rarawa) and Ngapaura Puatai (Ngāti Kurī) had three children: Kataraina (born between 1810 and 1820), Pinia (f) and Wata (m). Kataraina had four half-brothers and sisters (Hetaraka, Wi Patene, Meri and Te Waaka) from Honi Te Koni's marriage to Ani.

[9] Markham, E. *New Zealand or Recollections of it*. Wellington: Government Printer, 1963, p. 40.

[10] Murray, K J. *The Borrowdale/Murray Family: The Beginning of a New Zealand Dynasty*. Kaitaia: Top Print, 1988, p. 9.

[11] W B White, R.M., Mangonui, to The Under Secretary, Native Department. Reports from Officers in Native Districts, 18 May 1876, *Appendices to the Journal of the House of Representatives*, 1876, G-1, p. 18.

[12] Iehu Mumu Te Awha was also known as Raparapa te Awira and Te Huaki.

2

SON OF TE RARAWA, SON OF THE LAND

The family homestead was already home to five half-siblings from his mother Wini's first marriage, an older full-brother and at least two great-aunts when Hec entered the world. It would eventually house his parents, Wini's children from a previous marriage – Mary, Kate, Thomas Charles (Mick), Roa and Eliza (who Wini was carrying when she married Timoti) – and her children with Timoti – Hugh, Hec, Vera, Brown, Dixon and Monty, a whāngai cousin named Sid and up to three older relatives. Despite this imposing number of mouths to feed, the Busbys were reasonably well off by the standards of rural Māori in the district at the time. They lived in a superior dwelling, one of a dozen or so houses in Pukepoto at the time, and worked the land productively. Living conditions in the settlement had improved significantly for Māori since the first decade of the twentieth century, when, according to one eyewitness account there had been about twenty Māori families in the settlement:

> There was only one wooden dwelling – all the other natives living in raupo whares on the ground in most unsanitary

> conditions, and the greater portion of their papakainga was a wilderness of ti-tree, furze and rushes, only broken by a few cultivations of kumaras, taro, and maize, which latter as we all know was used as food in the form of 'rotten corn', that is, after having submerged in water until sufficiently decayed it was considered a great delicacy, especially with a piece of dried shark.[1]

The Busby residence, undoubtedly the 'one wooden dwelling' mentioned above, was a single-storey weatherboard house, constructed with pit-sawn kauri and featuring a gable roof and a long corridor down its centre. Several rooms branched off either side of the passageway. It had originally been designed as a two-storey home: the ceiling joists were solid eight-by-twos, and Hec remembers a space where the base of the staircase was meant to lead up to a second floor – which was never completed.

As far as Hec recalls, the outside of the building received not so much as a coat of paint, but a generous veranda welcomed visitors, and the interior walls were wallpapered. Just inside the front door hung a large framed photograph of the 1924 Invincibles All Black team, and more photographs graced the walls of the lounge, including a portrait of Hec's grandfather Mu, resplendent in a rugby jersey. The lounge also housed a gramophone along with a collection of imported records, mostly from Hawai'i, while a precious Golden Knight radio sat on a solid sideboard to one side of the room.

The master bedroom was located across from the lounge, which in turn led to a makeshift bedroom where two of the children slept. Further down the corridor were two additional bedrooms, and at the back of the house stood the kitchen which housed a long kauri table big enough to accommodate the entire family. A small room off the kitchen was used as yet another bedroom; here the young Hec and two of his brothers shared a double bed. Finally, behind the kitchen was the wash house and a porch that led to a clothesline and beyond that was a valley where a prolific orchard had been established. Fruit trees, including nectarines and white-fleshed peaches, provided a harvest that kept the family in preserved fruit and jam throughout the year. It was here, under the trees, that Hec and his siblings began their informal education, at the feet of their great-aunt Whenu. Chosen in her youth as a repository of ancient knowledge, Whenu was already in her mid-sixties when Hec was old enough to join the older children listening to her recount tribal histories. The narratives, including tales of Kupe and other early ancestors, would leave an indelible impression upon Hec, although they wouldn't gain real relevance for him until he had reached his early fifties.

It is not remembered how or where Hec's father, Timoti Iehu Busby, met Wini Rogers, a Pākehā from Kaeo who was six years his senior, but it is known that she already had four children and was carrying a fifth when she left her husband, Thomas Rogers, for him. Timoti had been just eighteen years of age when his father died, leaving him with the responsibility of heading the family and running the farm, but by the time Wini and her children moved in with him, he was an experienced farmer in his mid-twenties. By all accounts the couple were well matched, and according to Hec they shared a strong religious faith and a commitment to their family: 'We were a close family, and both of my parents ensured we got some moral grounding, both at home and through the local Rātana Church, which our family had converted to shortly after Mu's death.'

There was little or no paid work available in Kaitāia for Māori, especially as the depression years began to bite. The Busbys lived a largely self-sufficient lifestyle during Hec's childhood, relying on a little income from the sale of cream to the local dairy works to supplement the produce they grew in extensive gardens.

Like many rural Māori settlements at the time, Pukepoto had a community garden, where families grew kūmara, potatoes, corn and other crops. 'The only stores we used to buy in were flour and sugar, and a bit of butter when we weren't making it ourselves,' recalls Hec. 'We fattened up the occasional pig, and of course Mum would make wonderful Māori bread.' Wini was also a dab hand at growing strawberries, the proceeds of which paid for the family's first refrigerator and washing machine. Hec's eldest boy Walter remembers that 'she was the hardest worker I ever saw. She was tireless. I used to watch her digging in the garden barefooted with a spade. I'll never forget that.' Timoti was an equally hard worker; Hec's childhood memories of him paint a picture of a man who got the most out of the farm.

The gardens of Hec's youth sat on a parcel of land that bordered Lake Tāngonge, some 100 metres west of where Te Uri o Hina Marae stands today: 'It was a square 10-acre block off the main highway, and whoever wanted could plant a garden, big or small. There were no fences, but of course everyone knew their own plot. We had quite a big section of it, about 2 acres, because we used to grow enough to send sacks of kūmara south to family in Auckland each season.'

Working the gardens was extremely labour intensive in the 1930s and the family spent a considerable amount of time together planting, tending and harvesting their crops. It was also a period when the traditional ways were still taught, and as Hec recalls, the elders took special care to show the children how to plant kūmara according to old lore: 'We were only allowed to plant in the mornings, usually straight after breakfast, and we were taught to respect the sun. I remember we were never to face our backsides towards the sun when we were planting. When it came time to plant them we were told to always face the part that comes up like a hook towards the rising sun in the east. They even went as far as showing us how to hold the kūmara with our fingers a little away from the ends of the shoots, and then how to press them into the ground with the other hand. The final step was to cover the kūmara over with soil.'

In addition to home-grown fruit and various crops cultivated in the communal gardens, and kaimoana gathered from the coast, the family also enjoyed freshly shot kūkupa. Timoti, a crack shot with the rifle, would often lead expeditions into the forest behind his property to hunt the bird, and Hec thrived on the experience: 'Dad used to take Hugh and me up to hunt native pigeon, and over the years he showed us all of the old-time hunting grounds, as well as pointing out tribal boundary markers and the like as we came across them. The nights were usually pretty warm during the hunting season, so sometimes we used to sleep out, relying on a simple lean-to for shelter and a fire that would burn through the night.'

As they got older and more experienced, Hec and Hugh would sometimes head out hunting on their own, walking for miles over the hilly terrain: 'If there was a spare cartridge at home and we found it, we were off. You think about it now – one cartridge – and you laugh, but there you are. We loved hunting so much.' Later still, when Hec and Hugh's sibling rivalry started to turn more physical and their relationship became strained, Hec began to venture into the forest accompanied only by Hugh's sporting dog, Scott. They made a good team. The dog, untrained and usually overly excited around the farm, was a revelation in the forest. 'Scott would show me where the birds were,' remembers Hec. 'He would go along until he found some fresh bird droppings, then he'd turn around and look at me while wagging his tail.' Their best tally for a single day was twenty-two fat and succulent kūkupa.

Hec kept Scott's contribution to his success under wraps for as long as possible, but his father soon began to press him to explain how he was able to bring back so many birds. Finally he agreed to take his father out and let him in on his secret. The chosen day was cool and cloudy: the type of day, says Hec, that birds are often seen on the lower branches of trees. 'We were just going along and suddenly we came across Scott doing his thing, sitting below a tree, wagging his tail – and there was this bird sitting about 3 metres above the ground. Well, Dad couldn't get over it. I pleaded with him not to tell anyone, but of course within a week everybody knew about the dog: the old man couldn't help himself. After that everyone in the settlement raced to be the first to go hunting, because they all had to pass our home to get into the forest, and Scott would follow anyone with a gun.'

Balancing the thrill of the hunt were the day-to-day chores that all of the Busby children were expected to help out with around the farm. Hec's own introduction to mucking in came when he was barely five years old, helping his older siblings round up the family's herd of dairy cattle at daybreak and then again straight after school.

Although the family farm was never big enough to make a substantial return – running a mixed herd limited to around forty-five Jerseys and Holstein cattle at its peak – it did provide a little extra cash, and contributed to the larder. Milk was kept for the kitchen, and the skim from the vat was saved to feed the pigs and a resident flock of ducks. The rest, a solitary can of cream, was carried down to the farm gate, where it was collected each day.

As the boys grew older they started to help their father with more demanding work around the farm. Fencing was a time-consuming job, and drain digging was a particularly arduous task, given it was undertaken with shovel and spade. It was here on the family farm that Hec began to learn how to work horses. He started by ploughing the communal plot, under his father's watchful eye, and later graduated to transporting fence posts home from the forest on sleds. He was a keen student, and in his father he had the perfect role model: Timoti's skill at working horses was admired throughout the district, and had resulted in occasional contracts when the local council needed to employ the brute strength of working horses. 'Dad had the best team of working horses in the area,' recalls Hec. 'He got the contract to carry the pipes up when they put in the water pipeline from Ōkahu Falls to Kaitāia. It was a big job that lasted several months.' With many of the Far North's roads in a dire state well into the 1930s, especially during the winter months, teams of horses were often the only realistic option for moving heavy loads.

It was all hard, honest work that Hec grew to enjoy: 'I remember going up into the forest behind the homestead to cut pūriri for boundary fences. We'd cut down the trees using a cross-cut saw, and then split the logs using wedges and mauls. I can remember pulling on the saw. I really liked it. It was good healthy work.'

The manual work wasn't restricted to the males of the household however. Wini, never one to shy away from a job that needed doing, could often be found at the back of the house chopping iron-hard tī-tree for her stove. Planned or otherwise, it was perfect training for the wood-chopping competitions she later entered when the annual A & P show rolled into town. Hec: 'She would have been in her late forties or even older when she was competing, and she cleaned up. She was strong, and when it came to it she just wouldn't run out of steam.'

Wini's competitiveness and all-round work ethic would no doubt have impressed Hec's grandmother Raiha, who, aside from her midwifery and nursing duties, kept herself busy in the gardens where she could be found at all hours of the day, shuffling along the paths. 'She was of the old school,' Hec says. 'She couldn't sit still: fussing about in her garden and keeping an eye on the little fire she always seemed to have on the go for the weeds and leaves.' Raiha also spent time over the summer months at nearby Reef Point collecting seaweed to supplement her meagre pension. Hec and his siblings often joined her during the school holidays, staying over in a small tent that their father put up. A shelter belt constructed of sturdy tī-tree and an open fire completed the camp. Happy to be free from farm chores, the children helped collect seaweed and explored from sun up until sun down.

Raiha remained a link to the old customs until her death in 1948. She spoke very little English – a fact that Hec acknowledges is the reason why he and his siblings can all speak Māori – and she was central to one of the most vivid memories that Hec can recall from his childhood: 'One evening when I was about four or five my older brother Hugh and I were in our cot – top and tailed – ready for sleep, when an owl flew into our room through an open window. We watched it fly across the room and land on a coat hook, and of course we yelled out to the grown-ups. Raiha came running in to see what the commotion was all about, and we pointed up to the owl. As soon as she spotted it she rushed to try to trap it in the house, but as she was pulling down the window it escaped. Well, she burst into tears. When Hugh asked her why she was crying, she explained that the owl had come into the house to take our cousin's spirit away. She was looking after our cousin Ida, who was very ill at the time. I don't recall exactly what was wrong with her, but she died that night in the room just across the passage from us. She was only three.'

Hec's first and only school was a twenty-minute walk along the gravel road leading from Kaitāia to Ahipara. Like many rural schools at the time, Pukepoto Native School consisted of a single room with a porch, and was surrounded by a large playground of grass. A stand of acacia trees off to one side provided both respite from winter winds and welcome shelter during lunch breaks on summer's hottest days. It was here, during the first weeks of his schooling, that Hec was bestowed the name Hector (later shortened to Hec), by a Pākehā teacher who struggled to pronounce his name. Whether his parents agreed to the anglicised version of his name isn't remembered, but it soon stuck among his school friends.

Perhaps unsurprisingly for someone who freely admits to struggling through much of his classwork, Hec's memories from his school years are dominated by sporting successes rather than classroom accomplishments. Rugby was a popular pastime for both girls and boys during Hec's youth; children of all ages took to the playing fields at every opportunity. Hec, having inherited his father's solid build and showing signs of the determination that would be a hallmark of his adult years, loved the challenge of tackling the older boys. He also enjoyed the annual sports day held at Ryan's Paddock, a few hundred metres down the road from the school. By his own admission he wasn't blessed with the natural speed of his sister Vera, who was the school sprint champion, but he did have certain attributes that would prove beneficial later in life: strength of mind and a seemingly bottomless reserve of stamina. It wasn't long before he discovered that he could hold his pace longer than any of his peers, and he soon began to dominate the longer races.

It was about this time that Hec's parents began to organise occasional summer trips to Raiha's property at Aurere in Doubtless Bay.[2] Jack Walsh, who was married to one of Whenu's daughters, would pick up half the kids in the settlement, along with a few adults, and drive the ninety-minute journey in one of his buses to the banks of the Awapoko River. From there Raiha's brother William Piripi – generally known within the family as Piri Rou (and sometimes as Piri Piripi or Billy Darky) – would ferry everyone across to Raiha's land in his small dinghy. Hec recalls the river being full of fish at the time, and has memories of watching his uncle, Piripi Piripi, spearing flounder from the saddle as his horse walked through the shallows.

In later years Hec's parents occasionally travelled to the property to dig for kauri gum: 'From memory they only went there a few times to dig, but I remember at one point they probably stayed there for the best part of a month.' It was a 4- or 5-hour trip each way on the family's horse-drawn wagon and accommodation at Aurere was always basic: a tent would be enough in summer months, or, if Piri Rou was away on his travels, as he frequently was, they'd bunk down in his shed. Despite the hardships, the trip was always worth the effort; especially on one memorable occasion when Wini discovered a large chunk of ambergris (a sperm whale secretion) down at the beach that fetched £80 back in town.

Hec's mostly idyllic childhood wasn't to last, however. He was just seven when the Second World War erupted in Europe, and he can still clearly remember when the soldiers from Pukepoto came home for their final leave before going off to the war: 'It was a big event for the settlement, sending fifteen boys away, and the families got together to put on a supper and farewell dance for them at Te Rarawa Marae.' The lingering summer warmth of March 1940 was of little comfort for the families as they gathered to say goodbye to their sons. Most of the soldiers were single and aged in their early to mid-twenties and this was their final chance to visit with loved ones. In the morning they would be leaving Pukepoto to report back to the Māori Battalion at the Palmerston North Showgrounds, and soon after that they would be transported by train to Wellington, where the *Aquitania* waited to take them to war.

'None of my siblings were going,' says Hec, 'we were all too young – but a few of my close whanaunga were spending their last night with us. I wasn't old enough to ask, or even think about it at the time, but I suppose the reasons that they give for men going off to that war stood for our boys too: duty to country, but mostly for the adventure.' Despite the dangers involved, signing up for military service was undoubtedly an appealing option for many Māori in settlements such as Pukepoto. Opportunities for paid work in rural districts were few and far between; as a result, the chance to travel and to collect a regular wage was taken up by numerous young Te Rarawa men.

'Somehow I managed to stay up until the buses came at first light,' recalls Hec. 'The local dance band played through the night until the speeches started, although there weren't a lot of speeches really: I guess it would have been hard to find the right words at a time like that. But I can remember one of the fathers, Andrew Davis, who was about my own father's age, finishing his kōrero with a haka. It was such a powerful thing to see, the way he was doing it. It's still as clear to me as if it was done yesterday.' After the speeches the soldiers formed ranks and performed an impromptu march in the hall, Hec leading the men. 'I don't remember who told me to do it or why, but I can remember leading them around the hall just before the buses arrived.'

The morning was crisp and fine as friends and family filed out of the hall to form a guard of honour along the path to the road. Understandably it was a sombre scene as the soldiers made their way along the lines, shaking hands with each well-wisher. 'Then the buses arrived, already half-full with the Ahipara boys. We were all Te Rarawa and related, so they got off the buses and shook hands with all of our home people too. Then they all jumped on the buses – and they were gone.'

When the families went back into the hall Hec sat with the older men, as he often did, listening intently as they talked. He heard Piri Rou talk about the men who had climbed on the bus and then name those who wouldn't be coming back. 'And I know from my uncles he was right. Piri was picking out these guys as they were going around saying their goodbyes. Years later, when Piri was a very old man, I asked him how he knew who wasn't coming home. He told me he watched for the ones who cried as they were shaking hands: that was the sign.' One of Hec's uncles was among those named. Henare (Henry) Busby was just twenty-three when he died on 27 November 1941, far from home in the Western Desert.

With their young men away fighting a desperate war, communities up and down the country soon found ways to support them from afar. For the students of Pukepoto Native School, it meant making camouflage netting. Hec: 'We learnt how to make nets using needles and twine. The twine came in big rolls, and I remember that we had to pull it out from the middle of the roll to make sure that it didn't tangle. I don't know if other schools made camouflage nets as well, but we made quite a few, and we got pretty good at it too. We used the same knot they use for making fishing nets, and once each net was finished, we'd dye it in a big copper using strips of bark from the school's acacia trees to colour them brown.'

The children's contribution didn't end there though. As in many settlements during the war, the school became the focal point for much of the local fundraising effort, which often included concerts. The *Northland Age* reported on one such evening on 17 December 1940:

> Friday the 13th again found the Pukepoto youngsters in the field and quite undaunted by the reputation of the date. This time they gave a concert in the Rarawa Hall and their programme reflected credit on both themselves and their teachers. Later standards 1 and 2 presented a Nigger Minstrel show which was splendidly humorous as well as giving an opportunity for good singing. The evening was concluded by the presentation of 'Black Magic,' an uproarious farce which sent everyone gaily home from an evening long to be remembered. The total profits of the evening amounted to 8 pounds which is to be spent in sending parcels to the Pukepoto boys who are in the military forces.

The parcels, carefully wrapped in brown paper, contained chocolate, balaclavas, mittens and various other necessities. There was also a letter for each soldier from the children.

Although their minds didn't stray far from the soldiers fighting in North Africa and later in Europe, other more immediate concerns soon emerged among those on the home front. Japan had entered into the war and was rapidly advancing south, and German raiders – small, well-armed ships – were also becoming more active in the Pacific. Reports had started to filter through of the raiders attacking and sinking a number of unarmed merchant ships, as well as shelling Nauru Island in December of 1940.

Authorities in New Zealand summed up the possibilities of an attack on local soil and considered that a hit-and-run strike by a raider, or perhaps an aircraft-carrier-borne air raid, were the most probable forms of attack.[3] In an effort to reduce the chances of the enemy detecting coastal towns and cities, blackout orders for New Zealand were gazetted in mid-February 1941.[4] Hec remembers that the order was taken seriously in Pukepoto, and although few homes had access to electricity at the time, windows were covered and hurricane lamps were routinely dimmed. Schools were ordered to prepare for the possibility of an attack, and regularly practised emergency evacuation procedures. A single gas mask was sent to Pukepoto Native School for demonstration purposes and the children were taught how to put it on, but it was the only gas mask they saw for the entirety of the war.

Away from school, the Pukepoto community was actively preparing for any possible raid with a typical can-do attitude.

A kilometre and a half into the Herekino State Forest, up past the Busby homestead and along a track cut through gorse bushes, sat a newly constructed nīkau village. Positioned in a small clearing beside a stream, a half-dozen huts had been built to house a fleeing community in the event of a coastal attack. The structures, finished with gabled roofs of plaited nīkau leaves, had taken a mere day to complete, and were easily maintained. At the centre of the village stood a single padlocked wooden shed that held provisions, including tinned milk, tinned meat and quantities of flour and sugar. A number of elders, including Whenu, took the opportunity to sleep over at the village for days on end during the summer months, perhaps comforted by memories of living under nīkau roofs in their youth.

If large sections of New Zealand's population were feeling somewhat deprived when food rationing was introduced during the war, the Busby family weren't among them. They still lived largely off the land, growing a variety of vegetables and culling the odd cow for meat. Each autumn they would also kill a handful of pigs, which they boned and then smoked in the family kāuta – a free-standing fireplace behind the house with a corrugated iron chimney to funnel smoke up to the pork hanging above it. It was a simple but very effective structure. Seafood collected from Ahipara and surrounds also featured on the Busby table, although excursions to collect kaimoana were largely restricted to days when the tides were particularly low. During such times Hec recalls collecting kina and pāua in half a metre of water, and crayfish in little more than 2 metres of water.

Hec's great-great-grandfather Puhipi, photographed c 1850. Puhipi was a contemporary of the great northern chief Nōpera Panakareao and a significant chief in his own right. He was one of the few chiefs to speak in Kaitāia before the signing of the Treaty of Waitangi on 28 April 1840, challenging the British to explain how they expected to police the Far North from their Bay of Islands base. *Photo supplied by Busby family*

Hec's great-grandfather Timoti Puhipi and his second wife, Maata Mare. His first wife Marara had been taken in a typhoid outbreak that struck in 1874.
Te Ahu Heritage Archives, Kaitāia. A241/2

Hec's grandfather Iehu Mumu Te Awha. A keen rugby player, Mumu turned out regularly for the Kaitaia City Football Club. He was part of the 1903 team alongside representatives from other well-known families in the area, including the Robsons, Masters and Puckeys.
Photo supplied by Busby family

Hec's father, Timoti Busby
Photo supplied by Busby family

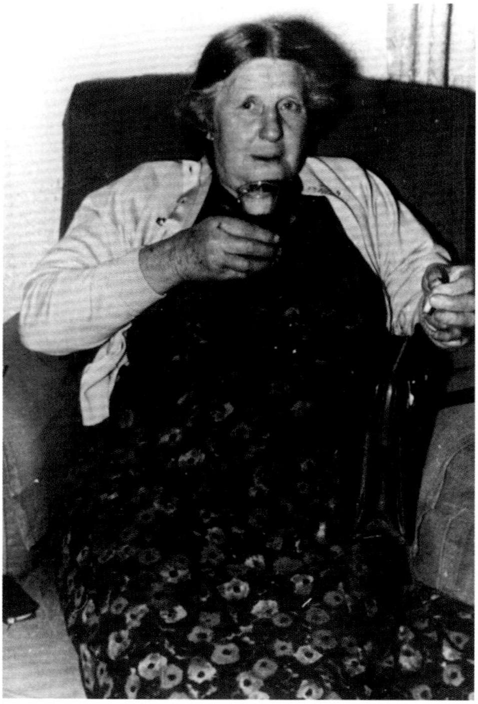

Hec's mother, Winifred (Wini) Ruth Busby.
Photo supplied by Busby family

Hec with his mum and eight of his siblings. Standing (l-r): Mary, Dixon, Eliza, Hec, Wini, Brown, Kate, Roa, Sid; with Monty kneeling.
Photo supplied by Busby family

Family photo taken at Ahipara in the early 1960s. Back row (l-r): Walter Tepania, Mrs Mary Tepania, Wini Busby, Timoti Busby, and Hec. Front row (l-r): Kathleen, Selwyn, Stephen, Hector Morris, Alexander (Alec), Kenneth, and Walter, holding Peter.
Photo supplied by Busby family

Hec with one of his workers, Jim Ritete, in the 1960s. Many of his workers remained loyal to him for years, appreciative of the regular work in a depressed region as well as Hec's 'work hard, play hard' attitude.
Photo supplied by Busby family

Hec performing the wero at the opening of Te Ohaki Marae, Ahipara, 1969. Hec picked up many tips relating to the wero from his mentor, Anglican minister Mutu Kapa.
Photo supplied by Busby family

Hec caught in full flight performing the wero on the Waitangi Treaty Grounds in the 1970s. His passion for tikanga Māori would later see him insist that traditional protocols were followed as closely as possible during the building of his voyaging and war canoes.

Newspaper photograph supplied by Busby family (newspaper source unknown)

On occasions the men would also try their luck netting, but it was always a challenge to get the fish back to their homes in good condition. 'There were very few cars around back then,' recalls Hec. 'In fact there were only two out our way, and neither of them were suitable for the beach, so if they wanted to take the nets out, they had to carry any fish they caught home on their horses. The problem with that was that many of the fish would get half-cooked by the body heat of the horses, and a lot were spoiled before they made it to the smokers.' It wasn't until suitable vehicles became more common that netting became popular among the Pukepoto families.

While Hec enjoyed visits to the beach to collect kaimoana, he had always preferred eeling in the local streams and rivers and along the edges of nearby Lake Tāngonge with his mates, especially during the long days of summer. Eel had been a staple food for many generations, but for the kids it was just about seeing who could catch the biggest one. The usual method was simply to put an arm down a likely hole in the riverbank and, when you found an eel, to wriggle your fingers past its head, grip its body tightly and ease it out. By the time Hec was seven or eight he was also beginning to hunt for eels at night, using a kerosene-soaked sugar bag stuffed into a 2-centimetre galvanised pipe, or torches made from strips of old car tyre, to light his way: 'You could practically eel all night with an old car tyre cut about half a metre long and 5 centimetres wide. It took a while to get it going, but once it was alight it was away.'

In early 1944 Hec moved a few kilometres down the road from the family home to live with his great-uncle Sam (Whenu's brother) and help out on his farm. His daily routine didn't change much during his three-year stay with Sam and his wife Alice, except that the walk to school and back was a little longer: 'I was only eleven when I took the place of my half-brother Mick, who'd been with them for a couple of years. They didn't have any kids of their own, so from being one of twelve it was suddenly one of one! I really enjoyed my time there, and both Sam and Alice were good to me.'

One of the benefits of Hec living with Sam and Alice was that they could occasionally afford to give him a few bob for the movies in Kaitāia. The bus fare from Pukepoto was two and six return, and entry into the Princess Theatre, then the main attraction in town, cost an additional one and six. 'The theatre was beautiful inside, with those flash folding leather seats. We'd watch anything, really, but our favourites were cowboy movies: Hopalong Cassidy, Roy Rogers, John Wayne and the like.'

Hollywood movies weren't the only new experience Hec had after swapping homes. Soon after he had moved to Sam's, his school started organising annual trips to the Treaty Grounds at Waitangi. The visits would become a pilgrimage of sorts for Hec, who spent hours sitting alone in the canoe house, mesmerised by the giant waka taua Ngātokimatawhaorua: 'You know, I thought it was just great. I'd stay there with the canoe for as long as I could, rubbing my hand along the carvings and wondering if I would ever see her in the water. It was the first time I'd ever seen a war canoe, and I thought it was the only one left – I didn't realise that Ngāruawāhia had waka as well. I don't know why, but I just wanted to be with it.'

The massive canoe, 35.7 metres in length, had been built for the 1940 centennial celebration of the signing of the Treaty of Waitangi, where she had been one of the main attractions. Soon after, she was dismantled and moved to a purpose-built shelter sitting alongside the carved meeting house Te Whare Rūnanga.

After the war, school fundraisers in Pukepoto switched from supporting the war effort to championing opportunities for local youth. These fundraisers continued to serve as an important social occasion for the wider settlement, and were often followed by a dance until the small hours. Music was usually supplied by the local Five Stars orchestra, and Hec himself was sometimes listed on the night's entertainment programme, singing either in a duo with Sammy Davies or in a four-part group that included Davies, Isaac Thomas and Mike Robson. Occasionally he also tried his hand at blindfold boxing, which was always a crowd favourite.

On one such night in December 1946, more than 200 people filled Pukepoto's Te Rarawa Hall to raise funds for the school's kapa haka group.[5] The rōpū was preparing to travel to Taipā to compete for the inaugural Tai Tokerau Shield on New Year's Day. The event, contested by school groups from across the Far North, would be remembered as a triumph for Pukepoto. After weeks of practice the group proudly lifted the shield, with Hec, as leader of the boys, standing centre stage.

It was around this time that Hec's brother Hugh contracted rheumatic fever, a serious illness that was infecting increasing numbers of children at the time. 'Hugh had three lots of the fever,' Hec recalls, 'and the doctors couldn't understand why he was still alive after the third bout. I remember them saying that he must have had a heart like an ox!'

While Hec managed to stay healthy, his commitment to school dropped away and it was no real surprise when he announced that he had had enough of school and intended quitting on his fifteenth birthday. He had done well at mathematics and excelled at woodwork, where he showed an immediate aptitude for the intricacies and skill required to complete complex joins such as the mortise and tenon, but little else in the classroom had caught his imagination: 'In fact my spelling and reading were pretty bad at school, and in some respects they still are. I really just didn't enjoy school.' His teachers had little to say when he informed them he wouldn't be returning after his birthday, and there was barely any opposition at home either. Hec completed his formal education at Pukepoto Native School with no qualifications. It was clear to all that he would need to make his mark in life, at least in the immediate future, using his hands.

Notes

[1] *Northland Age*, 9 July 1937, p. 8.

[2] According to tribal tradition, Raiha's property had been occupied by Māori for many, many generations: a fact that Timoti Wharemate Puhipi was aware of when interviewed by C F Maxwell, a sometime contributor to the *Journal of the Polynesian Society*. Timoti's narrative eventually made its way into Stephenson Percy Smith's *The Peopling of the North*:

> Timoti Puhipi says, that Tamatea, the son of Kauri was a chief of Ngati-te-Awa and occupied the country from Pukepoto to Aurere, including the shores of Ranga-unu Bay. He migrated southward for some reason

which is not quite clear, but was vaguely described as, 'He mate kino i pa mai ki taua iwi' (a great sickness which fell upon that people).

With reference to this mate or sickness, I may say that at Aurere, not far from Taipa, there used to be quantities of bones and skulls bare on the sandy flat near the river. I am told that this was a large kainga (village) of Ngati-te-Awa, but the people of the place were smitten with a strange disease, which appeared as black spots on the face and chest, and which killed very many of the inhabitants, in fact, so great was the mortality that the survivors fled panic-stricken, leaving the dead bodies unburied. These facts seem to point to some pestilence as having been the chief cause of the abandonment of the north by Tamatea's people. The reason of it, given by tradition, is witchcraft, as is often the case when anything happens that Maoris cannot readily account for. The plague is said to have commenced after a cannibal feast on some bodies which had lain for a considerable time in the summer sun.

[3] Taylor, N M. *The New Zealand People at War: The Home Front*. Wellington: Department of Internal Affairs, 1986, vol 1. p. 503.

[4] Ibid., p. 497.

[5] *Northland Age*, 13 December 1946, p. 5.

3

THE MAKING OF THE MAN

Having finished his schooling in August of 1947, Hec found work as a baker's apprentice alongside his brother-in-law Witana Wiki at the Rhys Williams Bakery. Newly built and featuring the latest commercial ovens, the bakery was situated on Kaitāia's main thoroughfare, at the corner of Empire Road and Commerce Road.

The hours were demanding for a fifteen-year-old, but Hec made a point of ensuring he was never late for a shift: he had, after all, milked cows at a regular hour, day in and day out, for the best part of a decade. His standard hours were from midnight until mid-morning Sunday to Wednesday, and from eleven on Thursday nights, when extra bread was baked for selling weekend loaves on Friday. To make sure he never missed clocking in on time, Hec moved in with his sister Roa and her husband Witana, who lived a few hundred metres from the bakery.

A fast learner under head baker Les Blyth's watchful eye, Hec was soon producing a range of small goods, including cakes, pastries and jam rolls – and although he enjoyed the work, baking never truly gripped his imagination. He craved something more active – and it wouldn't be long before such an opportunity arrived.

In December 1948 Hec took time off work to visit some of his old schoolmates working at the Portland Cement Works in Whāngārei. The city was a bright new world for a boy from the Far North, and Hec enjoyed the many social opportunities available. When foreman Harry Pitman offered him an entry-level job on the sweeping gang, he jumped at the chance. The work, mundane in the extreme, involved a never-ending round of sweeping up fine concrete dust, but it allowed him a level of independence he had yet to experience. To cut down on expenses, Hec moved into the staff accommodation block with his cousin Hoppa Simeon. It was a basic army-style set-up, with rooms off a main hallway and communal showers and toilets down one end, but it was clean and tidy, and, perhaps most appealing of all, it promised Hec a drastic change from living with family.

Hec's circle of friends grew as he became known about the cement works, but he spent most of his time off in the company of Hoppa, Barney Thomas (also from Pukepoto) and Dave Edmonds from Kaikohe. The four soon became inseparable, attending dances and frequenting The Settlers, where many of their fellow workers enjoyed a pint or two. Hec's tenure on the brooms was short-lived, however. After just three months his health began to deteriorate due to serious respiratory problems. When the company doctor determined that the cause was the inhalation of excessive amounts of concrete dust, Hec knew his fledgling career was at an end: 'I knocked off on his advice and went back to Pukepoto. To be honest I was glad to get home. I think I missed it a bit.'

Within weeks of his return home Hec and his cousin Sid had picked up seasonal work, clearing the 60 kilometres of drains that emptied Lake Tāngonge, alongside a contractor by the name of Dick Crbic. In particularly wet seasons the lake could flood and engulf farmland stretching from Pukepoto through to Awanui, and the water could stay up for two to three weeks at a time. The work started at Pukepoto and involved clearing weeds along the banks of the drains and in the waterways themselves with a hand-held slash-hook, and then pulling out the weeds and anything else they came across with a large hook.

The contract, lasting three months each year, was by necessity completed during summer, when the drains were at their lowest. It was hot, dusty and dirty work; Hec remembers that when they first started they would regularly suffer in the heat. It wasn't until Crbic got them into the habit of sipping cold tea that they managed to overcome the effects of the oppressive conditions.

Like many of his fellow Dalmatians, Crbic was a good cook who especially enjoyed pūhā and meat: a meal Hec and Sid also relished: 'He enjoyed his boil-ups, and of course that suited us just fine. He'd eat one huge meal in the evening and consumed nothing else but drinks of cold tea until dinner time the next day. We worked alongside him five days a week and we got paid well, but there was no mucking around – and we got bloody fit.'

Hec enjoyed the physical nature of the work, which also turned out to be perfect pre-season rugby training. Barely aged seventeen, Hec played hooker in the local club competition for the Te Rarawa senior team, which was made up almost exclusively of players from Pukepoto and Ahipara. The team's sometime coach, Moses Yates, had been a Northland rugby representative, and had also played rugby league for the Kiwis. 'He knew the game inside out, and had quite a calming influence on us,' recalls Hec, 'and the last thing he'd say to us before we ran out to play was always the same: if you have the ball, the other side can't score.' It was a logic that was hard to argue with.

There were two big matches for Te Rarawa every season while Hec was playing: one against Awanui and the other against Te Aupōuri. Awanui occasionally fielded All Black Peter Jones at lock and it was always a tough game when he was in their pack. 'Oh he was good all right, leading their forwards,' Hec says. 'We didn't beat them often when he was in the team, but when we did there was always a big celebration.' The second standout match, against Te Aupōuri, resembled a rerun of early tribal skirmishes at times and Hec was often in the thick of the action: 'There were always some shenanigans on the go in those games against Aupōuri, especially during away games, but it was, as they say, all left on the field, and Te Aupōuri, always the generous host, would invariably put on a good meal after the game. They were good times, win or lose.'

After a second and final summer clearing drains, Hec found full-time work labouring for Worth and Weber who had previously employed him between drain-clearing contracts, while Sid moved on to a firm in Kaitāia making and installing roof tiles. 'It wasn't long before Sid got me a job working with him,' Hec recalls. 'I would mix the mortar and Sid made the tiles: about 300 a day. Then, once the tiles were ready, we'd put them up. I worked there for about twelve months, only finishing up when I married my first wife and went gum digging at Pārengarenga in the Far North.'

It was also around this time that Timoti began to pass on what he knew about his family history and whakapapa to his second eldest son. Hec was the only one of his siblings who had shown any interest, and while Timoti didn't have a deep kete of knowledge to share, what he did pass on was eagerly absorbed. Timoti's own education in tribal matters had begun when, as a small child, he accompanied his grandmother Maata on horseback trips through Te Rarawa territory. Tribal boundaries, the names of abandoned pā sites, and other places of interest were pointed out as they were passed, and the recital of traditions helped pass the time.

One of the regular trips Timoti went on was the trek south to visit Taha, a sister of Whenu's, who lived at Koutu on the southern shores of the Hokianga Harbour. Hec: 'It was always an expedition of sorts, with horses needing to be readied and food and drink prepared and stowed away. The trip would take the best part of two days and included swimming the horses across Whāngāpē Harbour and a canter along Mitimiti Beach. They would leave the horses in the care of locals at Rangi Point, where the group would take a small ferry across the Hokianga Harbour.

The knowledge accumulated on such trips, and his attendance at many hui over the years, formed the basis of what Timoti eventually passed on to Hec: 'There were times when Dad and

I would sit down and he'd tell me stories about our ancestors, and about tribal events like the last war between Aupōuri and Rarawa – that sort of stuff. He spoke a bit about my great-grandfather and great-great-grandfather, but for some reason he never mentioned that they had been chiefs of Te Rarawa. I didn't learn that until quite late in life. But I did learn a lot of our proverbs from him – sometimes just by listening while he was practising his speeches out in the paddocks.' Whether he knew it or not, Hec was being groomed to head his family, and to lead his tribe – a calling that he wouldn't be asked to answer until he was well into his senior years.

By the time Hec had reached his late teens, he was a regular at local dances in and around Kaitāia. It was at one such dance that he was introduced to the woman who would become his wife. Like Hec, Kathleen Tepania came from a well-respected Te Rarawa family. Her father, Waata (Walter) Tepania, became the chairman of Te Tai Tokerau District Māori Council, a member of both the Tai Tokerau Māori Trust Board and the Te Aupōuri Māori Trust Board, and a member of the New Zealand Māori Council. Socially, Hec and Kathleen were well matched, and there was something about Hec's self-assuredness and good looks that attracted Kathleen to him. Before long they were an item, and within a matter of months they had announced their engagement. The only complication standing in their way was a clash of faiths. Hec, never deeply religious, soon cleared that obstacle: he renounced ties to the Rātana Church and was baptised into the Roman Catholic Church. Still only eighteen, Hec was now a married man.

Within weeks of the wedding, Walter Tepania asked the couple and Sid to join him and his sons, Ken and Eddie, digging for gum on the remote fields bordering the Pārengarenga Harbour. Although demand for gum was well past its peak, there was still a big enough market to allow a small, well-organised enterprise to prosper, and the Pārengarenga gum field was one of the few in the Far North that still had pockets of earth that hadn't been stripped bare.

The land they arrived at was harsh and unforgiving. Where great forests of kauri had once blocked out the sun, they found a desolate landscape pocked with gorse and secondary growth. Generations of farmers had struggled to make a go of it in the challenging conditions, and opportunities for non-farming locals were few and far between.

Unsurprisingly camp conditions were rough and ready. Hec recalls that there were a couple of huts for shelter, a galvanised tub to bathe in and a set of Coleman lamps for lighting. Beef stew and boil-ups cooked over an open fire featured regularly on the camp menu, and Hec himself added bread baked in a camp oven. He also brewed some potent beer, using a recipe he had learnt from his mother. 'We'd often drink it when it wasn't quite ready. Of course we tried not to, but at the end of a hot day the temptation was sometimes just too much, and after the first couple of glasses, well, away you go.' The one luxury they had, a radio, ran off a car battery, and allowed them to while away the evenings – keeping up with local and national news and listening to the latest dance songs. It was during their time at Pārengarenga that Hec's first son, Walter, was born.

The gum-digging operation, run under Walter's watchful eye, relied on a high-pressure hose powered by a V8 motor to slice into the peat. Hec: 'We set up our screen in a nice flat place and then worked away from it, cutting a V-shaped channel into the peat with the hose. Then we would peel off subsequent cuts, working away from the first cut to form an ever widening channel. The peat and chips would get washed down the channel to another member of the crew, who would shovel it onto the screen that separated the gum from the peat.'

The individual gum chips were then graded and bagged. It was a tried and proven system that produced good results: 'I can remember that first year we bagged 600 sacks of chips, and they were all trucked down to Houhora before being loaded onto one of the coastal ships. My father-in-law sold the gum to a company down in Auckland, who I think on-sold it to varnish makers. I don't even know how much money we got for all our work. I didn't worry about money too much then. All I know is that we got enough to get by on. It wasn't until after I started on the bridges that I began thinking about the future.'

The working week at Pārengarenga lasted from Monday to Friday, leaving the weekends free for hunting and fishing. On occasions the entire camp would walk down to a tidal river and net for mullet, but Hec's preference was fishing for snapper: 'The cotton lines we used back then were strong, and didn't cut into your hands like modern nylon does. The only thing about them was that you had to be careful to dry the lines after use, or the salt water would rot them.' Well looked after, cotton line could last for up to eighteen months.

Despite the abundance of fish and fowl in the area, a monthly drive back to Kaitāia was needed to pick up additional supplies for the camp, such as flour and sugar, oil for the lamps and occasional parts for the machinery. The trip into town also afforded Hec the opportunity to head over to Pukepoto to catch up with his family, and on occasion to attend tribal hui: 'I used to drive Walter and other kaumātua to hui whenever I got the chance really. Looking back, it was sort of an apprenticeship. I knew that my older brother Hugh wasn't interested in standing on the marae, and that it would eventually fall to me, so I took an interest from early on, and I ended up learning quite a bit about whaikōrero and other matters just by being there and taking notice.'

The foray into gum digging only lasted two seasons, due to a setback in Walter's health. Thereafter, Hec returned to work for Worth and Weber in Kaitāia, and moved his family into the back room of a billiard hall Walter had set up in Ahipara. 'It wasn't all that flash: the hall was originally an old marae building from Waimahana that had been dismantled and carried to Ahipara on the back of Walter's 3-tonne Bedford – but it was all we needed. It had a kitchen and a single big room where we all slept, usually with mattresses spread all over the place.' The billiard hall, quite the rural rarity, was open most weekends and the occasional evening when Hec decided he wanted to play. He had been keen at billiards ever since his bakery days, when he regularly played before his midnight shift commenced, and he was still quite the shark.

Once his health had returned, Walter began looking for a new business venture, and he settled on fishing the waters off Te

Rarawa's west coast. Never afraid to try his hand at something new, he set up a small commercial fishing concern at Wreck Bay, at the southern end of Ninety Mile Beach. He took on Hec and Ken as his workers: Ken and Walter manned the boat and Hec sold the catch from the back of an old blue Chevrolet. Hec's circuit took him from Ahipara through to Herekino, around to Broadwood, through the winding Mangamuka Gorge and finally back home, calling in on about forty families along the way and often not getting home until after midnight. It was an arrangement that suited him fine: by his own admission his sea legs were still several decades away.

As much as Hec enjoyed working for his father-in-law, he was aware that the work was largely seasonal. With a wife and young family to support, he was conscious that he needed a job that gave him the certainty of a weekly wage. In late 1950, Hec found a job with the Bridge Construction Company, a newly formed concern owned by Charlie Simelhay. Already in his fifties, Simelhay had worked as a foreman for Rope Construction building bridges, and with a bridge renewal programme under way in Northland, he saw an opportunity to stake his own claim. Hec's brother Hugh and cousin Sid joined him among the crew of eight.

Bridge building during the early 1950s was a slow and labour-intensive process. In practical terms it involved constructing a wooden frame, into which reinforcing rods were fixed and concrete poured. Once the concrete was set, the wooden frame was removed leaving the bridge in place. Hec: 'In those days we didn't even have the use of cranes. Everything was done by timber jack. Oh, tough work then, but it was good.

We were young and fit.' Completing a basic two-lane bridge typically took upwards of twelve months.

While Hec was a willing worker, his relationship with Simelhay was often tempestuous, and soon after they had finished their second bridge together, he quit. A stubborn streak, accompanied by an emerging desire to take charge whenever he saw workplace inefficiencies, had left him frustrated and continually at odds with his employer, so it was with some sense of relief that he finally returned to work for Worth and Weber.

His tenure there would only last three months, however. Simelhay knew the value of a man who could lead others, keep a project both on time and on budget, and be trusted to oversee what could be a complex piece of engineering. He asked Hec to rejoin his crew, this time as his foreman. The offer, which included an increased wage of £18 per week (the rest of the crew were earning £5 per week) was too good to turn down. Keen to ensure that Hec stayed with him, Simelhay also promised him a share in the business. On the strength of Charlie's word, Hec recommitted to the company.

His first job as foreman was the building of a one-way bridge just north of Ōkaihau. 'We were replacing the old type of bridge,' recalls Hec. 'A lot of the bridges in those days were basically pūriri decking across four girders bolted together with spreaders, even on the main highways. Of course I was really thrilled to be taking charge of a job myself, and it was easy as hell. I knew from then that I'd have no problems on the job.' Hec was still expected to do the same physical work as he had before, but now he had the added responsibility of making sure that everything was done to the required specifications. The new role gave him access to technical plans, which he would take home to study after work. 'I wanted to know all about bridge building,' he remembers, 'every little aspect. I was so keen I'd stay up half the night going over the plans, teaching myself the technical side of things.'

Soon after he returned to work for Simelhay, Hec decided to invest in some land. He had always been conscious of providing for his family, and had managed to save enough to purchase two residential sections sitting side by side in Ahipara's Teneke Road. The plan was to build a house there, in the heart of his tribal lands, and move in as soon as possible.

In April 1955, a couple of years after Hec returned to work on the bridges, his great-aunt Whenu passed away just short of her eightieth birthday. She had lived in the family home since before Hec was born, and had always been there on the periphery. She had been a voice of experience and, as many kuia have been, a holder of family and tribal knowledge. Hec was forewarned of her death in a manner that was becoming familiar: 'I was standing on the running board of my '41 Ford V8 truck watching a trawler fishing in Wreck Bay when, without warning, an owl came and tipped the side of my head. I tried to catch it as it flew through one window of the truck and out the other, but it was gone before I could get close.' Hec knew it was an omen, and immediately rounded up his family and headed for home. He was met on the road back to Ahipara by his brother Hugh, who gave him the sad news.

The years came and went while Hec continued to wait patiently for his partnership with Simelhay to be formalised, but it was never to be. Instead, Simelhay brought in an engineer by the name of Parkinson as a partner. Understandably, Hec was furious. He came from a tight-knit community in which a man's word was his bond, and he felt betrayed. Not yet twenty-five, he made a life-changing decision. He knew he could easily have fashioned a comfortable life as a well-paid foreman, but, spurred on by Simelhay's deceit, he decided to go into the construction business for himself. He was young and ambitious, and had the skill and confidence to take on jobs for himself. Indeed, he had been in a largely autonomous role for the last four years. In the absence of the promised partnership, and with a growing number of mouths to feed at home, Hec knew he would only really get ahead if he worked for himself: 'I was waiting for another contract to come up, and finally a little bridge at Ōruawaiti came up for tender. It was about 1958, eighteen months after Simelhay brought in Parkinson, that I went up against him and won the contract.' Upon hearing the news that his tender had been successful, Hec recalls with a laugh that he started to shake. In the shadow of the initial excitement was the realisation that he was grossly undercapitalised. 'Gosh, I was really worried. I had nothing other than the experience I had built up, a little cash in the bank and my truck. That was it. But I was determined to have a go, and that was the start of my contracting.'

Aged just twenty-six, Hec was in business. The first thing he saw to was securing a team of experienced workers. Sid and a couple of other labourers from Simelhay's crew followed him on his new adventure. Hec's father also joined the business, coming out of retirement to lend a hand. He was in his element working with his son, particularly when it came time to mix concrete. 'He just jumped on the back of the mixer, and he'd outwork guys half his age,' recalls Hec. 'He wasn't being paid, but he'd come along anyway to support me because he enjoyed the physical work.'

When he started on his first job, Hec knew that his biggest challenge would be driving in the foundation piles. Normally a contractor would employ a professional-grade winch to pull up a heavy-weight hammer, which was then dropped to drive the pile down. With precious little money in the bank, such an expensive purchase was out of the question. Instead, with his typical make-do attitude, Hec built a frame out of Oregon pine and bought a small friction winch, which he powered with a worn-out Model-A motor.

Given the nature of his equipment, Hec was understandably nervous when the time came to drive in the piles. Standing a little way from the action, he kept a watchful eye on the 3-tonne hammer as it was raised up the home-made rig. Everything had gone to plan so far: the materials had been purchased, and the winch had been looked over and was running smoothly. Then, on the very first drive, and with everything on the line, disaster struck: 'We were driving the very first pile and the damn thing blew to pieces. Jesus, you can imagine how I felt and the language that was flying around! I knew it was too light for the job, but I had my fingers crossed anyway.'

An inspection of the winch confirmed Hec's fears: it was beyond fixing. After the realisation had sunk in, Hec was jolted into action. He already knew that none of his immediate relatives had a suitable winch, and he didn't have the funds to purchase a sturdier model; he would have to look elsewhere to borrow one. His one chance was a casual acquaintance who had an old truck parked out the back of his house with a winch attached. Hec knew as he drove back to town that finding the winch in working order was a long shot, but it was his only hope. He hated the thought of having to go cap in hand to ask, but he also knew he had responsibilities. His work gang, each of whom had thrown in a stable job to come and work for him, were relying on him for a secure future, and here he was, watching as the dream of owning his own business dissolved before his very eyes. Fortunately the man was at home when he arrived, and, unbelievably, both the winch and the truck were still running. Hec was a relieved man when he finally watched the first piles being driven into place. The rest of the construction went to plan, and the bridge was finished on time and on budget.

However, things didn't get easier once the first bridge had been built. Hec still had the uncertainty of the tender process for future contracts to navigate, and he also had to replace his winch. To make things worse, he had already begun to build his Ahipara home when he won the Ōruawaiti contract, and he now had to sidetrack funds from that project to support his business. Luckily for Hec the second contract was a culvert, which required more muscle than heavy equipment: 'I didn't need to bring in any other machinery for the culverts, so that helped me along a bit, and there was enough of that sort of job to keep us busy.'

While the pressure of establishing a business was a constant drain on Hec's energy, he could at least take his family with him whenever he worked out of Kaitāia, putting a couple of army-style huts he had built to good use. 'It was good having my family there, better than being by myself – and at first living on the job wasn't all that different from living up in the gum fields really, other than we had young kids to look after.' Hec's son Walter has fond memories of the period: 'Dad taught me how to catch eels using a simple string and baited hook … well, blimey, I finally got one when he was building a bridge on a back road between Pēria and Victoria Valley, and I didn't know what to do with it!' 'Walter went haywire,' recalls Hec, who had to make his way down to the river to dispatch the eel before celebrating the capture with his young son.

When their third child arrived, Hec and Kathleen decided to rent local homes whenever work took them away from Ahipara, rather than use the huts. It was a convenience that they both began to enjoy: 'I was often on the job a long way from home for six to twelve months or more, so it was just easier to stay in a proper house rather than in the huts. For example, when we were building the Hūkerenui bridges either side of the railway crossing, we were there for about eighteen months in total.'

It wasn't until Hec's oldest child was nearing school age that completing the family house became a priority, and even then it was another twelve months before the house was habitable. Because much of Hec's contracting work was located out of the immediate district, he was limited to working on the house during the weekends. 'I was no carpenter, but I was handy with my hands, and learnt as I went. My half-brother Mick was a builder though, so occasionally I'd go and watch him at work and try to pick up a few skills. I built my own cupboards and stuff after watching him.'

There were just two bedrooms ready when the family moved in: Hec and Kathleen were in one room, and the three young children in the other. The kitchen and dining room were finished, but the living room was still a work in progress, as it would be for a number of years. Although the family were used to roughing it, living in an unfinished home proved far from ideal, especially as the children grew more active and began to explore every inch of the dwelling. Moreover, the pressure of the situation had a negative effect on Hec himself. A heavy sleeper in his youth, he was now finding himself lying awake at night wrestling to prioritise his spending: 'When I started contracting I would be up half the night thinking about how I was going to keep the business running, finish the house and still be able to feed my family. It was a very tough few years, but we managed to scrape through. There were plenty of times when I felt like chucking in the towel, but I suppose it was my stubbornness that kept me going.'

4

BUILDING A FUTURE

As a new decade dawned, Hec began to feel confident about his prospects. In just over two years his situation had changed dramatically, principally because he had taken control of his future. He had also been wise enough to learn from his time working under Simelhay. For instance, he knew where not to cut corners: 'Charlie was what you might call a penny wise and a pound fool. He didn't like spending money on his gear, and all for the sake of the cost of a new battery there would be three or four of us standing around for a quarter of an hour each morning while we were trying to crank-start the winch. I saw all that sort of stuff and I knew there and then that I wasn't going to do that sort of thing if I ever ran a business.'

While things didn't always run smoothly for Hec, two simple maxims that he followed throughout his construction career helped out more often than not: If you look after the pennies, the pounds will look after themselves, and There is no such word as can't. 'I really believe in that – there is always a way.'

And Hec isn't only referring to challenges on the worksite. He made a point of putting his workers' needs ahead of his own; an approach respected by his crew. In return, they gave their best to him: 'Looking back, I had to go without a lot of things myself in the first couple of years to ensure that I never missed paying my workers. And I tried to treat them right … If we were doing a concrete pour and they wanted to work like hell during the day, then we'd knock off early once it was finished – but I'd pay them for the whole day. I was happy as long as they did it right.' Hec would also pay wages if any of his workers had to attend a tangi – a courtesy that wasn't always afforded in the 1950s.

With his business well along the path to becoming established by the late 1950s, Hec was able to arrange an overdraft with his bank, thanks largely to guarantees provided by two local businessmen: shopkeeper Ivan Berghan, who came from an early missionary family, and electrician Keith Davan, who worked out of Kaitāia. This support was without question an acknowledgement of Hec's business acumen and an expression of his growing status within the business community. Together Berghan and Davan pledged to guarantee Hec for the not unsubstantial amount of £450.

Hec's family life was undoubtedly more settled now that the house was at least comfortably habitable, and he even began to take time off during Christmas breaks to relax: 'Every Boxing Day we'd load up my old army four-wheel drive and head off to stake our claim at Tanutanu Beach, down past Tauroa Point to the south of Ahipara.' While Hec pitched the tent the boys were sent off to collect driftwood for the first night's bonfire. For the children it was a week of adventure: exploring pools, collecting shellfish and fishing for rock cod with bamboo rods. For Hec, it was an opportunity to forget work and enjoy time with his family. They were simpler days, as Walter Busby recalls: 'When I look back, by today's standards it was a pretty basic life, but a good life. We were better off than most of the families in Ahipara, and we had lots of things to be thankful for, which is more than most people could say.' The holiday inevitably included a hāngī on New Year's Day, with mullet cooked whole, guts and all. It's a memory that still brings a smile to Hec's face: 'We'd just open them up and the flesh was beautiful, every time.'

Nothing of note occurred in the early years of the 1960s for Hec and his family until Hec's mother, Winifred Ruth Busby, passed away on 18 May 1963, aged just 64. She had been sickly in her final years, but the finality of her death came as a shock to the family. Hec was among those at her side when she took her last breath in the early hours of the morning. Minutes later, Hugh went outside and fired a shotgun into the night sky: a signal everyone in the settlement understood. Walter, a regular visitor to his grandparents' home, was deeply upset by the loss of his grandmother: 'It was pretty hard to accept it when she died. She was a big part of our lives growing up. We visited our grandparents most Sundays after church, and her passing left a big hole in our lives.'

In the months after Winifred's death Hec's father grew more and more introverted and he eventually chose to make a clean break and move to Auckland. As if the surprise of this departure wasn't enough, when news filtered back several months later that Timoti had met another woman in Auckland, the close-knit whānau back in Pukepoto were rocked. Walter: 'When my dad's father took up with another woman ... well, that had a big effect on me. I wasn't happy. My grandfather wasn't allowed to do that!'

By the late 1960s Hec had begun to feel the strong pull of his taha Māori – his Māori culture – and he started to spend more time in the company of his tribal elders. He had always wanted to learn how to speak on the marae, and because his elder brother Hugh was still largely uninterested in whaikōrero, he began to spend time learning the art from Kahi Harawira of Te Kao. It was an opportunity to build on the knowledge that his father had passed on to him, and also that which he had picked up while attending hui in the 1950s. He also began to study the art of the wero under the tutelage of Mutu Kapa, a respected kaumātua and Anglican minister: 'Mutu taught me some of the shortcuts in that game. He taught me to make sure that when I put the rākau down that my feet were positioned so I could start running immediately. And he told me to keep a special eye out for anyone from the manuhiri with bare feet, especially if there was a big crowd of people coming on to the marae. Any male with bare feet was a potential chaser, and they would occasionally hide among the visiting group to try and get the jump on you.' It was solid advice that Hec would remember whenever he was asked to perform the wero, including during the 1969 reopening of Te Ohaki Marae on Roma Road in Ahipara, and later when Queen Elizabeth visited Waitangi in 1974.

In time Hec became somewhat of an expert on the wero, and he developed a strong opinion about how challengers should behave when performing it, as long-time friend and Te Aurere crewman Marty Bercic explains: 'One thing Hec is not too keen on is when people sound like a rutting bull. The way he explained it was that someone doing the challenge, at least in the north, should be mimicking a fantail, and so their call should be high pitched. He also pointed out that the taiaha represents the tail of a fantail, and fantails are forever jumping and moving and flicking about, so the taiaha should never stop in one place.'

During this period, in the mid- to late 1960s, Hec learnt that a taiaha that had once belonged to his ancestor Puhipi was in the possession of a local Ahipara family. The background story, according to Eric Mathews, who had inherited the weapon, was that Timoti Wharemate Puhipi had given the taiaha to Eric's grandfather, Fred Mathews, shortly before Timoti's death, and it had made its way down through the family. By Hec's reckoning the weapon had been out of the Busby family's possession for some fifty-five years and he was keen to reclaim it. 'When I first approached Eric about the taiaha, I asked him what would happen to the stick after he went. He replied that he didn't know, but that maybe the right man would come along one day. So there and then I knew there was at least a chance that I'd get it back.'

Even so, the best part of a decade passed before Hec heard any more about the treasured weapon. One Saturday in 1973, the phone rang: 'It was Eric, and he said to me, "If you want the taiaha you'd better come and get it." And boy, I was out to Eric's place like a shot out of a gun!'

When Hec finally got his hands on the taiaha he found it beautifully balanced, but was surprised to find the surface carving on the weapon's upoko unfinished: 'It had two eyes dug out on one side, and one eye half dug out and one eye that hadn't been touched at all on the other. I think what must have happened was that Puhipi used it in a fight before it was finished, and it would have been too tapu to finish the carving once it had tasted blood.'

Hec's interest in carving had been growing ever since he had taken the opportunity to learn basic carving skills from noted Mangōnui carver Fred Broughton in the late 1960s. Broughton had been asked to oversee the replacement of several carvings that had rotted away over the years when the wharenui at Te Ohaki Marae was being restored. Hec's desire to learn all aspects of his culture, coupled with his inquisitive nature, soon saw him standing alongside Broughton, picking up some tips. Hec later added to these skills when he began to make taiaha and small pendants in the 1970s, and later refined them when it came time to work on larger projects.

About this time Hec also began to include his sons during his fishing and kaimoana-gathering expeditions, especially in the familiar waters along Ninety Mile Beach. One memorable day he recalls driving home along Tanutanu Beach with two of his boys, Walter and Ken, when he spotted a dark patch in the shallows. 'It looked like seaweed, but I had a feeling about it so I stopped the Land Rover and went down to have a closer look. It turned out to be a huge school of mullet sleeping in the shallows. We'd been out collecting kaimoana and I had all my gear in the back, so I grabbed my 25-yard net and I told the boys what to do. When mullet realise they're being surrounded by a net they head straight for the shoreline and try to escape around the ends of it, so I got the boys to hold one end of the net on shore and I carefully circled behind the fish. We were so quiet that we had actually encircled them before they realised what was happening. There were hundreds of them, jumping all over the place trying to escape.' Walter finishes the story: 'There were so many mullet that we had to use the incoming waves to help move the net up the beach, and as the waves went out again we were sitting on our backsides holding the net as best we could as it dragged us out!' The final count was sixty-three dozen mullet, most of which Hec and his boys distributed to family and neighbours on the way home. What remained filled the smokehouse for days and fed the family for months.

Hec also satisfied his appetite for diving the stretch of water from Ahipara south to the Hokianga Harbour during this period by completing a detailed survey of kaimoana stocks along the coast for the Tai Tokerau District Māori Council. Hec was the perfect person to take on the survey. He had dived the waters for crayfish, kina and pāua for years, and he already knew most of the areas where seafood could be found. 'My older boys and I surveyed the whole coast, marking what we saw on a chart. We must have plotted just about every rock that had a mussel on it, every crayfish hole, and where every kina and pāua was hiding.' It was one of Hec's key accomplishments for his tribe before he took on a kaumātua role in later years, and he was rightly proud of his boys' contribution to the survey.

In the meantime, however, Hec's home life was unravelling, and by late 1974 it was clear to him that his marriage was all but over. Kathleen and Hec's marriage had lasted twenty-four years, and had produced eight sons and two daughters: Walter, Kenneth Charles, Alexander John, Hector Morris,

Stephen William, Selwyn Mark, Peter Claude, Margaret, Moira and Robert Paul. The trouble, in Hec's eyes, was that Kathleen had become increasingly insecure with his spending more and more time away from Ahipara as local bridge-building contracts dried up. Hec was also frustrated by her lack of support for his cultural interests. 'We finally split up after I met Hilda Wilson [née Panaho],' recalls Hec. 'Hilda and I were on a number of committees together, and in the end we grew close because of our mutual interest in Māori culture.'

Hilda and Hec had first met in 1973, during the preparations for the 1974 visit of Queen Elizabeth II to Waitangi. Hec was representing Te Rarawa, and Hilda the Māori Women's Welfare League. If the attraction wasn't instantaneous – they were both married at the time – the respect they had for each other certainly was. They were both dedicated to working for the betterment of their people, and both refused to be sidetracked by petty politics or naysayers.

When the end of his marriage finally became a reality, Hec left the family home at Ahipara and moved into a flat in Whāngārei with a cousin. The decision to leave Kathleen opened the door to an enduring relationship with Hilda that was cemented when they moved into rental accommodation together just a few months later. But as that door opened, another began to close. Hec was never able to find a way to justify his leaving of Kathleen to his children, and the bond between them has remained strained. It is Hec's lasting regret that his relationship with his children has never fully recovered.

As their lives began to entwine, Hec began to actively support Hilda's work among the Māori communities in the north. It was an involvement he relished: 'Well, you know, I enjoyed all the time we spent on committees together, and helping Hilda out with her Māori Women's Welfare League and Kōhanga Reo work. I used to carry seating and marquees and all that sort of stuff on my trucks, so she could set up from marae to marae. We just sort of helped each other all the way through.' In return, Hilda began the often complicated task of putting Hec's business affairs in order, as Stanley Conrad, the son of Hec's lifelong friend Niki Conrad, explains: 'When Hilda came on the scene she soon discovered that Hec was running the business from his car boot. Hec knew what he was doing, but it wasn't the most efficient way to run a million-dollar bridge-building business. She tidied things up for him, encouraged him to invest in assets, and implemented some strategies to minimise his tax.' According to Hilda's long-time work associate and family friend Pita Paraone, her influence eventually extended much further than putting some order into Hec's business: 'There was no doubt that Hilda had a big effect on Hector, and Hector would be the first to concede that if it wasn't for Hilda he probably wouldn't have been able to achieve as much as he has.'

When Hec moved to Whāngārei, Hilda was working at the local branch of the Department of Māori Affairs as a Māori community officer. It was a role which was similar in many respects to that of a social worker, but in a Māori context; life experiences and people skills were the prerequisites for the job. Paraone describes the responsibilities of the job: 'Her work routinely involved enrolling people in boarding schools and getting scholarships to assist with the costs, putting people into homes, providing support for new mothers and getting them involved in community groups like the Māori Women's Welfare League. Later on she was also responsible for the whole Kōhanga Reo movement in Te Tai Tokerau, which meant ensuring that as each centre opened it was suitably serviced in terms of staffing and financial resources.' Hilda also had national responsibilities: she was the Tai Tokerau area representative on the Māori Women's Welfare League Council, and later a representative on the body overseeing the national kapa haka competition.

While Hilda's professional contacts would prove useful in a variety of ways, it was her access to information that Māori normally wouldn't see until it was too late that led to one of the most important contributions she made to the welfare of her people. Hec: 'Hilda's position working in a government agency meant that she was privy to imminent government policy changes that might disadvantage Māori, so with her help we were able to level things out a bit.' In particular, Hec and Hilda were able to keep a wary eye out for policy that might involve changes to the laws pertaining to tribal land. Joe O'Connor, who married into the family, explains: 'Hec learnt a huge amount about land issues, especially in regards to land around Pukepoto, because Hilda was in the right place at the right time. He had the information at his fingertips, and he brought that knowledge home and shared it. It was information that no one knew of until he told us. Now his mana is such that when a land hui is held in the north, his opinion is sought before anyone makes a move.'

Tribal matters weren't the only issue the couple dedicated themselves to. They continued to help with the running of

Waitangi Day celebrations after the Queen's visit in 1974, helping organise the event for another fifteen years. During the committee meetings that led up to the annual event, the force of Hec's personality regularly began to show through, as Pita Paraone witnessed on several occasions: 'Anyone who knows Hec knows that he doesn't suffer fools lightly, and he would become a little frustrated with a lack of decision making in the lead-up to the big day. You could always sense a change was coming as the meetings dragged on, and then suddenly Hec would be on his feet and we knew things were about to take a serious turn. That's when he would start speaking in te reo – and invariably that's when things started to happen.'

Hec's initial responsibility during Waitangi Day weekends was to look after Ngātokimatawhaorua and any visiting waka, but he was soon invited to sit on the paepae at Waitangi as well. Current Te Rūnanga o Te Rarawa chairman Haami Piripi: 'He has been there every year since I can remember, and he has been a strong supporter of the Treaty of Waitangi all the way through, to the point where Hector is now physically, spiritually and intellectually the guardian of the Treaty of Waitangi for Te Rarawa. He understands that the whole thrust of the 1935 Lord Bledisloe gift – the land, the resurrection of the Treaty House and the commemoration of the Treaty – is about the Pākehā-Māori relationship. Part of it is that he's really keyed into the legacy of our ancestors in respects to our future existence, constitutionally and as a nation. Everything he does is towards the theme of cooperation and mutual benefit, because our ancestors committed us to that. He's become a fine example of what a nation-builder should be, putting the foundations in place to take us forward. As his influence at Waitangi has grown over the years, he has become a focal point for drawing the strings together for Māori and Pākehā relationships, and sometimes that has occurred in situations where no one else could have done it but him, because of who he is and what he is. Part of it is the legacy thing, but he has to play his part, too, to understand his role. I can't think of anyone else who would be in that same category, and I have worked with a lot of prime ministers in my career. I don't know if he plays chess or not, but I bet he would be a fantastic player. He's often thinking five or six moves ahead.'

While the issues discussed at Waitangi are complex, Hec, true to form, manages to keep things in perspective when asked about his contribution on the paepae: 'My guiding principle is to fulfil the hopes of my tūpuna Te Ripi and Panakareao and to try to produce benefits for everybody. To me this means that we have to make our own decisions for today and for the future of our children. We have relied upon the decisions of our tūpuna to get us here, but now we need to rely on our own decisions to take us to where we need to go.'

Hec's presence on the paepae at Waitangi is one example of a large number of positions of importance that he has held within the wider Māori community. Despite his regular protestations over the years that he doesn't enjoy working on committees, he has accumulated a wealth of experience doing just that. In the early 1960s Hec started taking on roles in the Te Rarawa executive, the Ahipara Māori Committee and at the Ahipara Primary School, where he was the chairman of the Ahipara School Committee for a number of years. In the mid-1970s, he added to the list the chairmanship of the Waitangi Cultural Committee, as well as roles within the Te Tai Tokerau District Māori Council, the New Zealand Māori Council, the Waitangi Day Commemorations Committee, the Ngāti Kahu Trust Board and a number of waka-related trusts and federations.

While Hec's influence was increasing on the marae at Waitangi, Hilda and Kerewai Conrad were the undoubted driving force that kept everything running smoothly behind the scenes. Hec's cousin Robert Gable explains: 'Hilda and Kerewai did everything from purchasing the food to organising rosters for the boys to do the cooking and cleaning up. On top of that Hilda was also organising the cultural group for the ceremonial side of things on the marae. They were doing a tremendous amount of work.' Stanley Conrad, still a child in the mid-1970s, was another who witnessed Hilda working at Waitangi over the years: 'Hilda always made sure that the old people came first. She made sure they were there, and once they were that they were looked after. It was always the kaumātua and kuia at the top, then the paddlers, and then everyone else. That was her hierarchy. When she retired from the organisational side of things in the early 1990s there was a bloody big void, and no one could fill it. Lots tried, but by and large they all fell over.'

Hec's move to Whāngārei also gave him the opportunity to become more involved in kapa haka. His reintroduction to the art form had come during a trip to Tolaga Bay a few years earlier, where he had witnessed Prince Ferris leading a group: 'I went to the coast specifically to watch kapa haka because there was virtually no competition in the Far North at the time. When

I got there I saw a guy named Ferris leading a haka which had been written and composed by Sir Āpirana Ngata. It was all about Rūamoko, the god of earthquakes and volcanoes. Ferris's actions were exceptional and his voice was beautiful, and to this day I've never seen a man lead a haka as well as him.' The quality of performance and intensity of competition captivated Hec, and memories of his own participation in kapa haka as a child came flooding back. He sought out and joined the Taki Rau Māori Group, under the tutelage of Winiata Morunga. Marty Bercic, a junior member active in the group when Hec first joined, recalls Hec's involvement: 'Hector actually used to compose haka back then, and he also co-composed a number of waiata with Winiata. I think it would be fair to say that at that time Winiata was more the musician and Hector was more involved with the lyrics, especially the links to karakia and traditional sayings.' Hec also stood in as male leader on occasion, a role he relished. Later he became a kapa haka judge at the local level, a position he fulfilled for several years.

Soon after resuming his performing career Hec successfully put his name forward as the Tai Tokerau delegate to the New Zealand Polynesian Festival (now Te Matatini), which organised the biennial national kapa haka competition. After two financially draining festivals in Rotorua, the national committee sought expressions of interest to host and run the 1975 festival. The Tai Tokerau committee – with which Hilda was heavily involved – jumped at the challenge, and submitted the winning proposal to have the festival in Whāngārei. The decision to pitch for the festival wasn't, however, universally supported. Reverend Kīngi Īhaka was at the forefront of the challengers, demanding to know how the Tai Tokerau committee expected to make money in Whāngārei, when there was no money to be made in Rotorua. It was a fair question but, as Hec remembers, one that ruffled a few feathers: 'He was from up here and he never had faith in his own people. We knew we could succeed though, and in the end we made quite a bit of profit: $40,000, I think.'

Hec's main job in the lead-up to the festival was to organise the construction of the stage for the Ōkura Park event. Complicating matters was a pre-booked athletics event that wasn't scheduled to finish until a couple of days before the festival was due to open. With access to the infield out of the question during the track meet, the only feasible option for Hec was to build the stage clear of the athletic track and move it into position on the eve of competition. Not for the first time, he called on his long-time mate Dave Culham of Culham Engineering to help out. Culham provided beams to form the frame of a 12-metre stage, onto which a series of 6 x 4-foot plywood sheets would be fixed. Rollers and a winch truck enabled the stage to be moved into place relatively easily. It was a simple and sturdy platform, and everything went smoothly at the festival, recalls Hec, other than the moment when 'one big bloody hori jumped through the plywood! I think it was a crook bit of ply, but still …'.

Hec's enduring involvement in kapa haka – from schoolboy competitor to judge; event organiser to regional representative – was eventually recognised in 2002, when he was bestowed life membership of Te Matatini. His selfless work for his people had also been noticed throughout the north, thanks in no small part to the exposure afforded by his support of Hilda. His reliability and hard-working nature gave his kaumātua the confidence that he could be trusted with positions of importance. Hec's emerging interest in waka taua would offer the perfect avenue for him to prove himself even more thoroughly.

5

REBIRTH OF A WAKA NATION: NGĀTOKIMATAWHAORUA

An encounter with the massive waka taua Ngātokimatawhaorua, whether she's in the water or at rest in her shelter, is the highlight for many visitors to the Bay of Islands. Commissioned for the centenary of the Treaty of Waitangi in 1940, she was originally intended to be one of a pair of waka to be paddled during the commemorations. The second, to be named Mataatua, was never built.

The building programme was started in 1937, when three logs were felled in Puketī and Omahuta Forests, both of which are located inland from Kerikeri. Among those engaged to build Ngātokimatawhaorua was Tom Munu, a relative of Hec's who had been brought in to work under master carver Piri Poutapu. Munu helped with the shaping of the hull, and was ultimately responsible for carving the waka's tauihu.

The canoe was the first major waka constructed in the district for more than a century. She was finished late in 1939, but her launch, which had promised to be a momentous occasion, was soon causing headaches when the assembled crew couldn't move the waka from her resting place. Whina Cooper witnessed their attempts:

> The idea was to pull the canoe along the rollers, using the winch and human labour. But when they tried to, it wouldn't budge. It just stuck fast, in spite of all the helpers and the wire ropes and everything. So they stopped trying and the old people had a conference about it. Te Puea was there, and said to them, 'Never mind the winch. That's all wrong. That's what's holding it back. We'll do it the Maori way.' So one of the tohungas, Pita Heperi, got up on top of the canoe and recited a karakia. Then he began a tauparapara and as he called out – jumping back and forth – all the Maoris pushed. Over the other side of the creek some old ladies began to call it to come forward. And do you know it did, it just slid beautifully down the slope and into the water like a swan. Old Heperi, dancing up and down it, waving his taiaha and calling out, didn't look like himself at all. He was taken over by his tupuna and became one of them.[1]

The 35.7-metre long canoe, finally afloat but sitting alone without Mataatua, was paddled by her seventy-strong crew from Kerikeri to Waitangi, where she stole the show during the centennial celebrations on 6 February. The event, described enthusiastically in the *New Zealand Herald* the following day, was witnessed by an estimated ten thousand Europeans and Māori. The newspaper went on to detail the appearance of Ngātokimatawhaorua and a second waka taua, built by Ngaituteauru carvers, at Hobson Beach.[2] Special mention was also made of the presence of two platoons of the Māori Battalion who acted as the guard of honour to receive the Governor General, Lord Galway. Later in the day, when the soldiers were ferried to Ōpua to board their train for Palmerston North, they were escorted by the two waka taua. It would be the last time the canoes would be seen together on the water for seventy years.

Shortly after the celebration, Ngātokimatawhaorua was disassembled and transported to a custom-built canoe shed sitting alongside the meeting house Te Whare Rūnanga in the Treaty grounds. This would remain her permanent home for the next thirty-three years, until, in 1973, it was suggested that the canoe be refloated for the forthcoming visit by Queen Elizabeth II. The canoe's involvement in the commemoration, it was argued, would allow Māori to showcase their unique culture to the world's media. Hec, as a member of the Te Tai Tokerau District Māori Council, was heavily involved in discussions, and was delighted when the proposal went ahead. He saw past the marginal benefits of putting the waka on show however; his wider vision was the possibility of using the relaunch as an avenue for the revival of waka culture in the north. A committee was immediately established to oversee the relaunch. Hec's good friend Niki Conrad accepted the honour of captaining the waka for the Queen's visit: he had been a member of Ngātokimatawhaorua's crew when it was launched in 1940 and was one of only three crew members from that launch to return in 1974. Allan Karana was placed in charge of the training regime. It turned out to be an effective partnership.

With the decision to relaunch agreed to in principal, Hec brought in one of his trucks and cautiously moved Ngātokimatawhaorua from her canoe shed to Hobson Beach. The ageing Piri Poutapu was then invited to travel to Waitangi to look over the waka; the committee wanted to know if the canoe was still seaworthy and, if not, what could be done to prepare her for use. Things didn't go strictly to plan however, and a group of eager locals, perhaps conscious that there was little paddling experience in the north and that the Queen's arrival was looming, decided to launch the waka early rather than wait for Poutapu's arrival. With the help of rollers and, according to the *Northern News*, 'about 200 men, both Māori and European',[3] she was launched and taken for a short paddle. When Hec heard what had happened, he was furious, and drove to Waitangi from his home in Whāngārei to confront the men: 'I really went off the handle at them. I wasn't there five minutes before I jumped in my truck and headed back home.'

With the waka already afloat, Poutapu's visit never eventuated, and by the time Hec had calmed down and returned to Waitangi the following weekend, the canoe had been readied for another outing. The plan was to paddle her from Hobson Bay across to Russell and back with a full complement of eighty-three crew. Hec, although still simmering, agreed to join the crew.

What started off as a comfortable paddle on flat water soon turned into an emergency. Not even halfway across to Russell, Ngātokimatawhaorua started taking on serious amounts of water through the haumi joins in the hull. Hec would later say that his being on the waka at that time was a stroke of luck: 'It was a good thing that I was on the canoe when it was swamped, because I saw then that it was as safe as a bloody church. The water level reached the top of the gunnels and we just sat there. We didn't sink.' Even so, eighty-three men and boys sitting in a partially submerged waka in busy waters was far from ideal. What could have become a maritime disaster was only averted when the paddlers were able to hail a passing launch and have the waka towed to shore.

During an investigation into the events of the day it was determined that the canoe hadn't been reassembled with the same care and diligence that the original craftsmen had afforded her, after she was moved to her shelter. On top of that, the thirty-plus-year-old muka packed between the haumi joins to stop water seeping into the hull had broken down.

The committee insisted that the waka be relashed before it was taken out on the water again. This time, Hec called on Tom Munu for advice. Despite being 'as good as blind', Munu was able to pass on a few important tips, as Hec explains: 'Tom showed us how to lash properly and how to make sure the haumi joints were really tight. He started by lashing the top two holes on each side of the hull, before lifting the end section of hull up so he could pack fresh muka into the joint. When he had the required amount of muka packed in, he eased the end back down, which crushed the muka in position. I saw straight away how effective that way of doing it was, but it was one of those things you might not work out without a lot of trial and error.'

Despite the early setbacks, Ngātokimatawhaorua's eventual role in the 1974 celebrations was enthusiastically observed by officials and the public alike. With white-tipped paddles flashing in unison over the calm waters of the bay, the waka taua was undoubtedly an awe-inspiring sight for those on land. Her relaunch was greeted with tears of joy among many of the kaumātua and kuia in attendance, and the general public was equally as enthralled by her presence – especially those who watched her making her way out to the Royal Yacht *Britannia*.

The giant waka was entrusted to convey Prime Minister Norman Kirk and Minister of Māori Affairs Matiu Rata from the Waitangi jetty out to the Royal Yacht, where the two men witnessed the Queen signing the amended Royal Titles Act. In an act of nationalism, the Act dropped the reference to the 'United Kingdom' in the title of the monarch of New Zealand.[4]

After the signing, the official party boarded the Royal Barge, which made her way to shore in Ngātokimatawhaorua's company. Hec: 'A couple of weeks before the big day they told us that the Royal Barge would be travelling at a steady 6 knots, and of course we had to keep up with her if we were to escort her in. Well, from the outset we realised that it was going to be a challenge for us. We had done a few tests, and had never gotten past 5.5 knots, and even that was only for a short stretch. On the day though, Ngātokimatawhaorua was flying – so that shows you the ihi of the person. We maintained 8 knots all the way in, and they actually had to speed up to stay with us.' Undoubtedly this was the first time the majority of those in attendance had seen a war canoe in the water, and Ngātokimatawhaorua was a worthy recipient of applause and cheering from the huge crowds who had travelled to Waitangi for the Queen's visit.

Back on shore, Hec participated in the wero for the official party. His part in the challenge, which according to Haami Piripi is still remembered on northern marae today, culminated in Hec rolling his taiaha down his extended arms and catching it in his mouth. Hec explains: 'A fairly old guy from down the East Coast taught me that move, and it didn't actually take too long to perfect it. One of the secrets he told me was to fashion a taiaha with a rounder shaft than normal, so that it would roll better.' Soon after the wero Hec and the others involved in the challenge were introduced to Her Majesty: 'She asked if I had a connection to James Busby, to which I replied that there were no bloodlines: that Puhipi had taken the name when he was baptised. She had plenty of time to talk, and actually seemed quite interested.'

As Hec had hoped, Ngātokimatawhaorua's performance had inspired many of those who paddled her to pledge themselves to further training and future outings. A new canoe shed – Te Korowai o Maikuku – was built at Hobson Beach, and plans were put in place to take her out on a regular basis. It was also decided that a dedicated caretaker should be appointed to watch over the waka. Hec was given the honour. One of his first tasks was to undertake a comprehensive inspection of the vessel. He already knew that the crew was finding the canoe difficult to turn, and he was determined to find out why. When he pulled out his builder's string he discovered the problem: the stern was 20 centimetres out of alignment. The simple remedy was to shave around half a centimetre off one side of the haumi join where two of the hull sections met. It wasn't a major adjustment, but Ngātokimatawhaorua was a national treasure and belonged to all five tribes of the north – it was a symbol of their strength and mana – and Hec wanted the reassurance from Tom Munu that his solution was the best option before he cut into her. Hec: 'When Tom came to Waitangi to check out the canoe for me he started by walking around the canoe, feeling it with his fingertips. Then he stood at the prow and looked down its length as though he could see the other end, which was kind of funny because he was practically blind by then. Even so, he had felt the joins and he knew they weren't quite right.' Munu agreed with Hec's proposed course of action, and told Hec that he had the authority to do whatever needed to be done with the canoe. It was, recalls Hec, reassuring to hear.

As Hec's experience working on the canoe increased and his confidence grew, his leadership skills, already strong after two decades of managing men in his own business, began to show through. Pita Paraone describes Hec's approach: 'Even back then, when he spoke about waka everyone listened. It didn't matter whether they were older than him or younger; every single person listened because they respected that he was the one bringing that kaupapa back, at least in the north. And he's never been afraid to delegate to those who wanted to be heard, so to speak. He would give them that responsibility. I suppose that aspect of things was all part of his master plan: to ensure the required skills, whether related to leadership or maintenance, were passed on to the next generation.'

One such example of Hec's forward thinking involved the choice of material when it came time to relash the canoe. Rather than selecting the long-life nylon rope recommended by others, Hec insisted on a rope with a medium-term lifespan; it would need to be replaced every few years. 'That is the foresight of the man,' says Paraone. 'Where someone else might think that he should use a material that would last for as long as possible, Hec could see that if he chose a long-lasting rope his knowledge of lashing would probably be lost. Instead he wanted to keep the skills alive through regular use.'

As well as promoting the cultural and physical elements of waka, Hec has been able to use waka to help a number of individuals living on the margins of mainstream society over the years. 'Hec has had a very positive influence on a number of people,' continues Paraone, 'some of whom may very well have gone off the tracks if it wasn't for Hector and his willingness to bring them on as part of the waka kaupapa. He has the ability to see something in them that a lot of us can't see, and that's the sort of ability that few have: being able to recognise the hidden potential in people. Some of those young men in question have gone on to make a positive contribution to society because [with Hec] they've learnt discipline and how to follow instructions and what it means to be part of a team.'

One such recruit that Paraone and a few others wondered about was a heavily tattooed gang leader who started training with the crew during the lead-up to Prince Charles and Princess Diana's visit in April 1983. Although his commitment to training was clear, his police record nearly saw him barred from the waka. Hec: 'The police went through the crew list a day or so before we were going out, and they immediately put a cross against this guy's name. They told me that they didn't want him on the waka. Well, I got a bit of a shock, really. I thought about it for a while and I decided that I had to stand up for this guy. I knew he was trying his best to get back on the straight and narrow, and that pulling him from the crew would ruin him, so I told them that if he wasn't in the crew then the waka wasn't going out. I told them that I had enough faith in this guy, and that I was 100 per cent confident he wasn't going to play up.' Despite their doubts, the police ultimately relented, and no incidents occurred. Indeed, by all accounts the royal couple's outing went without a hitch; video footage from the day shows a delighted prince and princess sitting amidships as the waka glides across the flat water to Hobson Beach, New Zealand's flag flying high from its taurapa.

Later that day, after Ngātokimatawhaorua had been settled in her canoe shed, Hec and Niki Conrad departed Waitangi and set out on the long drive north to Te Kao. The next morning was the opening of the duck-shooting season, and they were both keen to get a good night's sleep at Niki's home before the traditional dawn start. Hec's sleep was broken in the early hours of the morning, however, by an urgent phone call from Pukepoto. His father had passed away, aged seventy-nine. 'After I got over the shock of the news I decided to stay at Niki's rather than return to town. I knew I couldn't do anything there and then, so I thought I'd see if I could bag a couple of ducks before I went back. But, by gosh, I never hit a bloody duck that entire morning.'

Timoti had been a beloved patriarch of the family and a respected elder of his people. 'He was,' remembers Joe O'Connor, 'an astute gentleman, similar to what Hector is today: a bit of a perfectionist, and staunch in his tikanga and history. When I first met him he was getting on in age, but even then – I don't know how to put it into words – he was *there*, and you knew he was there. He had that presence about him.'

Hec, Timoti's second-born son, would in time follow his father's footsteps and become the head of the Busby whānau, but before he could ascend to that role, his growing profile would see him come to the attention of several kaumātua as he proved himself at a tribal level. Among them was the respected Tūhoe elder John Rangihau, who would introduce Hec to the man who would change his life.

Notes

[1] King, M. *Whina*. Auckland: Hodder and Stoughton, 1983, pp.143–4.

[2] *New Zealand Herald*, 7 February 1940, p. 13.

[3] *Northern News*, 10 January 1974, p. 6.

[4] The Royal Titles Act changed the wording for the title for the monarch of New Zealand from 'Elizabeth II, by the Grace of God of the United Kingdom, New Zealand and Her Other Realms and Territories Queen, Head of the Commonwealth, Defender of the Faith' to 'Elizabeth the Second, by the Grace of God Queen of New Zealand and Her Other Realms and Territories, Head of the Commonwealth, Defender of the Faith.'

6

A LINK TO ANCIENT KNOWLEDGE

If Hec's divorce and relocation to Whāngārei made the mid-1970s a period of turmoil, the 1980s were memorable for a number of positive events that would shape his later years. While he would continue to oversee Ngātokimatawhaorua, fate was charting a series of parallel courses that would eventually see Hec gain prominence on both the national and the international stage. Hec's influence wouldn't be restricted to such lofty heights, however. His construction know-how and access to heavy machinery and the occasional truckload of surplus materials allowed him to help out on a number of community projects in Pukepoto and Ahipara, and sometimes further afield. Among these were much-needed upgrades to the facilities at both Te Ure o Hina and Te Rarawa marae, and while Hec didn't always have the opportunity to help in person, he always ensured that whatever supplies he could get hold of, such as reinforcing rods and cement mix, were available when they were required.

His help also extended to organising carvings; if he couldn't produce them himself, then a deal was always to be made.

Hec: 'When we were about ready to start on the carving for Te Poho o Ngāti Kahu meeting house at Pēria, my son Robert, who was going to oversee the carving, got an opportunity to travel to America that he couldn't turn down. It was horrible timing for us, but he had to go. That's when master carver Takirirangi Smith came on the scene. He had brought a group of students up north to watch kūaka leave on their migration to the northern hemisphere, and he dropped in to my home to introduce himself while he was up here. He told me that he was hoping to take some of his students to observe the kūaka arrive at Saemangeum in South Korea, one of their stopover points during the long flight back to their nests in Alaska. Well, at that time I was trying to work out how I'd be able to get twelve poupou carved for the Pēria Marae, so I made him an offer. If he carved the poupou we'd pay $1,000 for each carving as long as the funds went towards his students' travel expenses, and that is what happened. He completed the carvings and the students went on their trip.'

During the 1980s, Hec's gift for healing began to emerge. 'It all started unexpectedly, during the 1983 Christmas break-up party at my depot in Kaitāia,' recalls Hec. 'A young guy came to me and told me his brother was sick, and it sounded like some of the old mākutu business – a curse of some sort. Well, I knew that Tūhoe kaumātua John Rangihau was coming up to see me later that week, so I told the boy that I had the very man to help his brother, and that he would be arriving on New Year's Eve. He didn't think his brother would last that long, and that's when it all just came to me. I sent my son Alec to a freshwater spring up behind the family property at Pukepoto to fill a half-gallon jar, and when he got back I drank a bit of the water and did a karakia over the rest. Then I told the boy to wash his brother's head with a cupful from the jar and then have him drink some.

'The next morning I rang Alec and asked him to check on the boy for me. When he rang back he told me it had been the first night the brother had slept for over a week, but that wasn't the only news he had for me. My son Hector Morris had been in a car accident that same night. Fortunately he was okay, but straight away I had a bloody feeling that it had something to do with what I'd done. When I finally got to speak to John Rangihau about it he told me that the first thing I needed to do whenever I got involved in healing was to protect my family with a karakia. It was a lesson I never forgot.'

While the sudden onset of his ability to heal was unexpected, Hec took it in his stride. He had grown up in a community where such things weren't unheard of, and as a child he had been introduced to the supernatural through tales told by his elders. One such story, told to him by an uncle, sticks in his mind: 'From what I can gather, there was a meeting at the marae in the early 1920s where they decided that they should tidy up the cemetery. One of the things they had decided to do was to pull down an old vault that held some remains and a few precious taonga. It was tapu work of course, so they asked an old tohunga named Maka Pera to oversee things. On the appointed day the men he had chosen for the work gang assembled outside the cemetery gate while the tohunga recited a karakia. Then, shortly after they started work, one of John Borrowdale's sons, John Murray, arrived at the cemetery gate. The tohunga walked up to him and asked him why he had come, as he hadn't been invited. Murray replied that he wanted to lend a hand, and then walked straight past Maka and started to help pull down the vault.

'Well, nothing untoward happened during the rest of the day until they were walking back to the marae. The track down from the cemetery wound past the stream that runs through Pukepoto, and as they walked by one of the deep pools Murray seemed to get pulled towards the water. The men around him could see he was trying to hold back, but a taniwha got hold of him and dragged him to the stream, and he was soon under the water. A couple of the men jumped in to save him, and when they pulled him out they discovered that one of his eyes was missing.' According to Hec's uncle, Murray had been dragged under by a taniwha named Paraweta, and losing his eye was the price he had to pay for intentionally interfering with such tapu work.

Hec accepted his newfound power with equanimity, but was nonetheless comforted by the knowledge that John Rangihau was there in the background to guide him in such matters. Indeed, in the ensuing years John Rangihau would become an important source of support for Hec, passing on much of his knowledge; particularly in regards to tikanga. 'John Rangihau would come and visit me and we'd talk for hours at a time about all sorts of things, and it wasn't until later when I started thinking back that I realised that e tohutohu mai ana ia i ahau – he was tutoring me.'

Rangihau's influence over Hec's future took a significant turn in late December 1983, when a slightly built Hawaiian arrived at Hec's Doubtless Bay property. Although Hec couldn't know it at the time, his visitor was to have a profound impact on his life.

The introduction had been orchestrated after John met with members of the Polynesian Voyaging Society while passing through Hawai'i. The Society had been formed in 1973 by Hawaiians Tommy Holmes and Herb Kawainui Kāne and American anthropologist Ben Finney. The initial aim of their fledgling society was to build a voyaging canoe capable of testing whether or not Polynesian ancestors could have navigated the vast distances between Hawai'i and eastern Polynesia – in effect, whether they were able to settle the far-flung islands by design rather than accident. After the successful maiden voyage of their double-hulled waka Hōkūle'a to Tahiti in 1976, the society went through some heartbreaking times: a second voyage to Tahiti was aborted in 1978 when the Hōkūle'a capsized near Lāna'i and crew member Eddie Aikau was lost at sea. However, by the mid-1980s they had recovered, and were in a strong-enough position to start sharing their voyaging expertise throughout the Pacific.

Indeed, at the time of Rangihau's visit, the Hawaiians were in the process of planning their 1985 'Voyage of Rediscovery', a journey that would see them call in at numerous islands. Because Aotearoa was tentatively included in the itinerary, the society asked Rangihau where the canoe's navigator, Nainoa Thompson, should base himself to study the stars. Rangihau considered the options for a moment before recommending Hec's Aurere property. He knew of Hec's interest in waka, and he recognised that the remote campsite would offer an excellent base to study the night sky.

The then twenty-nine-year-old Thompson's sojourn in Aotearoa didn't start off as smoothly as he had hoped it might, however. Recalling his New Year's Eve arrival, Nainoa says: 'Well, I flew in to Auckland and expected John to meet me at the airport and take me up to meet Hec, but he was nowhere to be seen. It turned out that he'd had to return home at short notice to attend a tangi, and so instead he'd arranged for one of his acquaintances to meet me. All of a sudden I saw this very friendly lady holding a banner with my name on it. My first thought was that things weren't going to be as straightforward as I had imagined.'

The drive north to Hec's property added five hours on top of the long flight from Hawai'i, and Nainoa's travel-worn appearance wasn't improved by the stretch of unsealed road that he still had to negotiate. 'I jumped out of the car at Hector's gate and said my thank yous, then started walking along this long and dusty road to Hector's caravan, carrying my luggage – it's maybe a couple of kilometres from the main road. The next thing I knew Hector was driving up behind me with his truck and fishing boat, and telling me to jump up on the boat trailer. I jumped up, and immediately I heard something on the trailer break. Nothing was said, but I had the distinct impression that Hector blamed me for the breakage. I don't know if he was just in a bad mood or didn't really want me there, but by the time we arrived at his caravan I was feeling pretty uncomfortable. I introduced myself to him and told him why I wanted to study the stars. I think John Rangihau had told him a little bit about me, but only that an Hawaiian wanted to come and look at the stars, and I think that's all he knew at that stage.'

As Nainoa remembers it, the initial meeting between the two men was somewhat of a tense stand-off, until one of Hec's companions eased the situation by making small talk. Then Hec demanded that the Hawaiian point to the north. Nainoa admits the cool reception and direct question had him momentarily flustered: 'But I concentrated and finally got a reasonable idea of my position, and I managed to locate north. Well, Hec was sort of standing behind the boat by this time, and I think he was checking his compass against my directions, which were pretty accurate. I didn't hear exactly what he said, but he mumbled something, and one of the boys took me to stow my gear.'

Fortunately the tension softened later that night when Nainoa dropped back to the caravan to wish everyone a happy new year. Hec and some of the others were sitting by the campfire having a few drinks when he arrived. 'Suddenly Hector got up and he started to speak to me in Māori.' The Hawaiian didn't understand what was being said, but felt the emotion of Hec's speech, and remembers seeing tears running down the older man's cheeks in the light of the flames. When he finished speaking in te reo, Hec switched to English, saying: 'In this land, we still have our canoe buried. In this land, we still have our language, and we trace our genealogies back to the names of our ancestral canoes. But we have lost our pride and the dignity of our traditions. If you are going to bring Hōkūle'a here, it will bring that back. Whatever you need to do, I am with you all the way.'

Nainoa was glad for this change in attitude; an important aspect of his visit was to determine whether he could become spiritually grounded in Aotearoa, and Hec was the perfect man to help him achieve that grounding. Hec's connection to the Far North and its history was undoubted. His ancestors had occupied the land for many, many generations, and the mana of influential chiefs pulsed through his veins. He also had close ties to the land he now owned: it was the land that his grandmother Raiha had owned, and that he himself had played on during summer trips as a child.

Nainoa's stay at Aurere lasted two weeks. Each night Hec would drive him to one of a series of locations where he could study the stars. His primary aim was to view the star patterns from the northern limit of the land. The stars would be the key to him finding land should he voyage to Aotearoa; ultimately, they would help him judge how far south he was. 'I concentrated on the shape of the sky to the north of Aotearoa because our strategy for the voyage was to sail to the east of the North Island and then turn in towards it. I was looking for stars that were just cresting the northern horizon, because I knew that should I sail for Aotearoa those stars would help me to judge when I had sailed far enough south to turn towards the North Island.'

Nainoa's first-choice location was Te Rerenga Wairua (Cape Reinga), but intermittent cloud cover made it difficult for him to see the night sky clearly there, and the bitterly cold winds at the Cape tore into him. Although they soon decided to abandon the Cape, the drive north presented Hec with the opportunity to guide his guest down a cliff to a small cave where he had earlier discovered a series of markings carved into the rock. He had often wondered whether they might possibly relate to the stars. Stepping into the cave, Hec pointed out a line of three marks that he thought might represent Tautoru: Orion's Belt. Nainoa: 'It was a little difficult for me to decide if they were constellations, as it was quite dark in the cave, but what was important to me was that from that moment I understood how deep [knowledgable] Hector already was, in terms of the traditions of voyaging and his people's connection to the heavens.' It was a pivitol moment in the relationship. Nainoa had found a kindred spirit in Hec, and Hec had found a man who would inspire him to lead a renaissance in his home waters.

In the following days, Hec drove Nainoa to Ninety Mile Beach near Waipapakauri, and to the shores of the Hokianga Harbour. 'We went to the north, east and west coasts to see the stars on each horizon,' recalls Nainoa. 'The shape of the sky here in Aotearoa is so different from Hawai'i, and you can't even see the key northern stars that we use for navigating from down here, so I had a lot to learn. Even the most southern of stars that we can see from home are in a different position when viewed from Aotearoa.'

While they were driving from one location to another, Nainoa began to ask Hec about local history. Hec could answer a few of the Hawaiian's questions, but there were significant gaps in his knowledge. 'I was actually quite embarrassed. I had always been keen on tribal history and whakapapa – the only one in our family really – but when I started contracting on the bridges it used to muck me up sometimes. I couldn't concentrate properly on my work, because my whakapapa studies kept coming back to me. It got to the point where I had lists of names and other stuff constantly running through my head, so I had to make the decision to put my books to the side and leave it alone.'

Thanks in part to Nainoa's questions, the tribal traditions recalling the history of the land and the deeds of his ancestors began to come back to Hec – but it wasn't until Nainoa returned the following year that the depth of Hec's reclaimed knowledge became evident. 'He drove me to the museum in Kaitāia and when we arrived I asked the curator some fairly specific questions. The curator couldn't help me, but Hector could. It was then that I realised that this man has an incredible capacity for understanding his culture and its history. Way more, in fact, than the guy who was paid to do that job. Hec was a walking, cultural historian.'

Hec's time in Nainoa's company had piqued his interest in migration traditions, and he was soon reading anything he could get his hands on relating to the subject. Unsurprisingly, his study sometimes resulted in more questions than answers. For instance, Hec couldn't work out how, according to some traditions, the navigators who arrived on the east coast of Northland could use Venus, the setting sun and Atutahi to guide them to Aotearoa. It wasn't until he plotted the voyage on a chart of the Pacific that he found the answer: 'It turns out that in November the latitude where the sun sets and where Venus sinks below the horizon is virtually the same. Once I knew that, it all clicked. For the first half of the trip to the Kermadecs they used the sun to steer by day, and by night they followed Venus. Then, when they needed to change their course to a more southerly heading, down to the North Island, they started to use Atutahi.' For Nainoa, Hec's explanation was a revelation: 'Back then I really didn't understand that myths could make a valuable contribution to voyaging. I was there to study the stars with a more mathematical – perhaps scientific – mind.'

As Nainoa's first visit came to an end, Hec drove him down State Highway 10 to Waitangi, where John Rangihau would pick him up and drive him the rest of the way to Auckland for his flight home. During the drive, Hec pledged to do everything he could to help the Hawaiians. 'When Nainoa first started to tell me about the plan to sail Hōkūle'a through the Pacific on their Voyage of Rediscovery he still wasn't sure whether they would come to Aotearoa. The heavy seas and cold conditions were a real concern for them, so I really put the pressure on him ... kia haere tika mai ki konei ... I told him that so many people were non-believers when it came to our ancestors and their navigation skills, and that the only way to stop that kind of talk was for his canoe to sail down to Aotearoa. I told him that I would be 100 per cent behind them. If they came I would look after the crew from the moment they got here, and I'd look after Hōkūle'a when the crew returned to Hawai'i to wait for the next sailing season.' Nainoa, moved by Hec's impassioned plea, finally relented and agreed to add Aotearoa to Hōkūle'a's itinerary. Hec departed Waitangi in tears.

It wasn't until after Nainoa had returned to Hawai'i that Hec began to fully understand the extent of the young man's voyaging experience. At the time of his first visit to Aurere, Nainoa had already established himself as the primary navigator for Hōkūle'a, having learnt his skills directly from Mau Piailug, the famed Micronesian master navigator from the Caroline Island group. Nainoa had started as a deckhand on the return leg of Hōkūle'a's maiden voyage between Hawai'i and Tahiti in 1976, and had been captivated by the experience. But the catalyst for his decision to learn traditional navigation was the devastating loss of his mentor Eddie Aikau in 1978.

What was supposed to be a triumphant rerun of Hōkūle'a's 1976 voyage quickly turned into an emergency when, just hours after leaving Honolulu's Ala Wai Harbour, Hōkūle'a's starboard hull flooded, and the vessel was swamped. Worse was to come, however; around midnight a rogue wave struck and flipped the double-hulled canoe. Somehow all sixteen crew members were accounted for in the 6–8-foot swell, and they managed to stay with the canoe throughout the night. The next morning, with Hōkūle'a drifting further and further from land, and having received no response to their calls for assistance, Eddie Aikau volunteered to paddle a surfboard the 12–15 miles to Lana'i for help. Eventually Hōkūle'a was spotted by a passing plane, but despite an intensive search and rescue operation, Aikau was never seen again. Nainoa: 'My commitment to becoming a navigator didn't come until Eddie was lost. I had never believed I could be a navigator. I had met Mau and he was magical, and I thought I could never be like him. Everything changed when we lost Eddie though. I knew that I needed to do whatever it took to fulfil his vision of pulling Tahiti up out of the sea. That is when I was committed.'

Nainoa immersed himself in the renaissance of Hawaiian culture during the ensuing years, and he became more involved in the revival of voyaging. Both his father and maternal grandmother had worked tirelessly for their people in social services, so it wasn't surprising to those that knew him that Nainoa should eventually follow in their footsteps, utilising waka culture to try to reconnect his people with their ancestors, and, more importantly, to their ancestors' values. In an interview for the *Vaka Moana* exhibition curated for the Auckland War Memorial Museum, he crystalised his thoughts: 'We sail because we believe that voyaging canoes have a role in today's society, based on keeping us connected to who we are today in the twenty-first century; by clearly knowing who we were and where we come from. In the absence of that understanding, we have no identity – we have no distinction, and to be homogenised into the rest of the world would be a cultural failure.'[1]

Once it had been confirmed that Hōkūle'a would sail to Aotearoa, Nainoa returned to Doubtless Bay several times during 1984 to continue studying the stars and to strengthen his relationship with Hec and the land. He was also keen to enlist a local to join his crew for the leg from Rarotonga, principally to act as a guide when the vessel reached Aotearoa, but also so that the Hawaiians could begin to share the experience of deep-sea voyaging with Māori. Hec immediately recommended Stanley Conrad, whom he considered the perfect choice. Although he was still young, Stanley was well regarded among his people, and had been on or around the ocean for most of his life. 'Where I come from there was only about 40–50 kilometres between the Tasman Sea and the Pacific Ocean, so we were always in touch with the sea as youngsters,' says Stanley. 'I had also been part of Ngātokimatawhaorua's crew since I was a little fella, progressing from bailing the canoe to paddling, and on to commanding a section of the waka.' Conrad's education on the water continued during school holiday breaks, when he was recruited to help on his father's commercial fishing boat: an experience that would eventually lead to a career in commercial fishing and his captain's ticket. 'After a few years commercial fishing out from Nelson, I returned home to run the old man's fishing business in the north, so I was pretty familiar with the coastline that Hōkūle'a was going to encounter when she arrived in Aotearoa.'

If Stanley was the obvious choice as far as Hec was concerned, it is probable that Nainoa was a little less sure when he arrived at Niki Conrad's farm to meet him. 'The first time Nainoa came to meet me I was right smack in the middle of a tiff with my sister. She was going down to the beach wearing a yellow bikini with a little frill and she looked stupid, so I called her a bloody big jumbo, and that started her off.' The argument had started in the kitchen and ended out in the yard, with Stanley's mother Kerewai trying to break up the fight with a broom. 'There was dust flying in all directions and the chickens were making a hell of a racket in the pen – it was bedlam,' recalls a laughing Stanley.

Once the dust had settled, Hec introduced Nainoa to Stanley and his parents. Hec explained to the Conrads that the Hawaiians were looking for an experienced local to join their crew for the leg from Rarotonga, and that he thought Stanley would be perfect for the role. Niki, while conceding that his son fitted the bill, wasn't initially keen on him getting involved. He was wary of putting his son's well-being in the hands of a man he didn't know, and was also still a little unsure of the voyage's purpose. It wasn't until Nainoa explained the goals of the voyage in detail that Niki and Kerewai began to understand why Hec was so enthusiastic about including their son. Stanley: 'As Nainoa explained the reason for the voyage, my dad began to get the whole picture. But even then he was reluctant to let me go; he was concerned about all those things parents worry about.' As for Stanley, he was more interested in the free flight to Rarotonga than the voyage itself. 'I said yes straight away, just to get out of Te Kao. My only thought was that there was a free plane ride and everything paid for, because it would be my first trip overseas. I didn't even know how far Raro was, but it was an opportunity to get away and see something new.' In the end Niki relented and agreed to allow his son to participate in the voyage. It would be a decision that would not only change Stanley's life, but also usher in a new era of voyaging among Māori in this most south-western of Polynesian islands.

Notes

1 *Vaka Moana: Voyages of the Ancestors*, exhibition DVD. Auckland War Memorial Museum, 2006.

7

HŌKŪLE'A: A GIFT FROM THE GODS

Hec's commitment to supporting Nainoa was consolidated after he and Hilda travelled to Hawai'i at the invitation of Nainoa's father, Myron 'Pinky' Thompson, in 1984.

It was during this first visit that Pinky inquired about Hec's name, remarking that 'Hector Busby' didn't sound very Māori. 'So I showed him my passport and explained that 'heke' means to migrate, 'nuku-mai' means to come closer together and 'ngā iwi' means the people. That's when he looked me in the eye and told me that I was not there by chance, that I was on a mission. To be honest I didn't think too much about his comment at the time, but as the years have gone by, it's become clear to me that he knew exactly what he was talking about.'

Pinky also asked Hilda to visit some of the local 'Aha Pūnana Leo, the Hawaiian equivalent of Kōhanga Reo, during their stay. She was immediately struck by the lack of spirituality in the preschools, which, she decided, was caused by the lack of Hawaiian language in the curriculum. She also noted that the teachers taught like they were in a public school setting, rather than in the whānau environment embraced in Aotearoa.

With Hilda as his unofficial consultant, Pinky went about reinventing the ʻAha Pūnana Leo, incorporating many of her recommendations along the way. Hec and Hilda's short stay left a lasting impression on the pair; particularly Hec, who had been captivated by the whole experience. He returned home with plenty to think about. His next visit to Hawaiʻi, in May of 1985, was timed to coincide with Hōkūleʻa's departure on the Voyage of Rediscovery. Nainoa had requested Hec attend the formal departure ceremony, where he would recite Māori karakia to protect the vessel and her crew during their epic adventure. The waka had already sailed successfully to Tahiti and back twice (in 1976 and 1980), but this would be her most demanding voyage to date. Her twin crab claw sails would need to drive her through challenging seas, and the strain on the ten massive cross-beams holding the hulls together would be more than they had ever endured. As far as the Hawaiians were concerned, Hec's contribution was more than mere window dressing.

A few days before the historic voyage Hec joined Hōkūleʻa's crew as they sailed from Honolulu to the Big Island. The trip was rough but exhilarating. Hec: 'That was the first time I had been on a voyaging canoe, and it was actually a little bit scary! Mind you, there are some rough patches in the channels between the islands, and we had spray from the waves breaking over the prow that was thrown way over the stern. When we finally got on the leeward, sheltered side of the Big Island, we had a comfortable sail down to Miloliʻi, the fishing village where they were leaving from. Even though it was rough I thought it was great.' Importantly, Hec's time on board showed him how seaworthy double-hulled canoes could be. As he had done when Ngātokimatawhaorua took on water crossing the Bay of Islands, Hec took confidence from Hōkūle'a's performance; particularly her stability in rough waters.

This trip also presented Hec with an opportunity to meet Mau Piailug, another voyaging icon who would have a profound influence on his life. Mau had been brought up on his native island of Satawal in the Caroline group of islands, learning the arts of traditional navigation at his grandfather's side. He learnt how to use the stars, sun, winds, clouds and the swells and other clues from the ocean itself to guide his waka, and in the evenings he absorbed waka lore listening to the village men tell stories of sailing and navigation in the canoe house. Now in his early fifties, Mau still had the typical stocky build of his people, but the muscular physique he had once sported was softening, and a new pair of glasses featured above his wide smile.

Mau had first come to the attention of the Polynesian Voyaging Society in 1973, when Ben Finney began searching for a traditional navigator to guide the Hōkūle'a on her maiden voyage to Tahiti. It had taken some effort to find a suitable navigator, but after talking to Mau through an interpreter it quickly became obvious to Finney that he was the perfect candidate. Not only did he have the experience and temperament required, he was also willing to share his knowledge with outsiders. Nainoa would later acknowledge that it was a fortuitous coming together: 'He was probably the single individual in the world who had the skill, knowledge and experience to make the cultural jump so that all of us could truly learn enough to do it ourselves.'[1]

The fact that Mau was willing to pass his knowledge on represented a major break from the customs he had been brought up with, but he well understood that his form of navigation would in all probability die with him if he didn't share it with outsiders. He had been conscious for some time that the majority of the young men from Satawal were leaving the island, mainly for education and economic advancement. Of those that remained, most were indifferent to learning traditional navigation, and the rest weren't up to it. They were desperate times.

Hec's stay at Miloli'i stretched on as Hōkūle'a's departure was delayed by contrary winds, and it was looking more and more likely that he would miss the departure completely, due to pressing work commitments back in New Zealand. Fortunately for Hec, Pinky found a solution: 'Thankfully Pinky was able to bring the ceremony forward, and I was able to recite my karakia over the canoe and crew a few days before they actually set sail. It was a shame I had to leave, but I was happy that I was able to do my bit for the Hawaiians.'

The trip had been yet another positive experience for Hec and he boarded his flight consumed with the possibility of replicating the Hawaiian programme back home. After seeing the cultural benefits Hōkūle'a brought the Hawaiian people first-hand, he was convinced a similar waka-based programme had the potential to benefit Māori. Even so, it was a bold ambition for a man who had yet to build any sort of waka, much less a double-hulled canoe capable of surviving in the southern Pacific Ocean.

Any such ambition was put aside however, when, barely a week after returning home, Hec suffered a perforated stomach ulcer. According to the doctors at Whāngārei Hospital he was lucky to survive the day: had his arrival been delayed by as little as an hour, it's likely that he wouldn't have lived through the ordeal.

While Hec lay in hospital recovering from his operation, Hōkūle'a was under sail, making for Tahiti. The voyage south would take thirty-three days, and be followed within days by the shorter leg to Rarotonga. An eight-week break followed, before the crew, including a wide-eyed Stanley Conrad, would assemble in Rarotonga. Nainoa had scheduled their departure for late November, to ensure it coincided with the traditional sailing season for voyages to Aotearoa.

The sail plan would see Hōkūle'a sail south-west for the Kermadec group of islands, before changing course and heading directly for the Bay of Islands on the east coast of Northland. The Kermadecs, sitting 520 miles north of Aotearoa, are an acknowledged signpost for navigators using traditional navigation methods, and their position significantly reduces the possibility of navigator error. 'The reason,' explains Nainoa, 'is that when you leave Rarotonga the angle to Aotearoa is quite fine, but once you get down to the Kermadecs you are so much closer, and the angle widens considerably.' In effect, any traditional navigator worthy of the title should be able to find Aotearoa from the Kermadecs with relative ease; indeed, numerous modern-day voyages guided by traditional techniques have proven this to be correct. Supporting the theory is the fact that the Kermadecs are well documented in a number of Māori migration traditions. It is remembered, for example, that the Kurahaupō was nearly lost near the island group after lashings holding her hull timbers in place were damaged during the voyage to Aotearoa.[2]

One of the numerous learning opportunities Stanley Conrad was provided with on Hōkūle'a culminated in his being the first among the crew to sight the Kermadecs. Although he didn't yet have the voyaging experience of his crewmates, in retrospect he is able to recall several clues in the lead-up to his sighting that hinted that land was in close proximity. The first came when Hōkūle'a encountered a large pod of sperm whales to the north-west of the Kermadec islands. The whales were travelling north along one of their main migration paths past the North Island's East Cape and along the Kermadec Trench. The next clue drifted in on the breeze the evening before land was sighted; Stanley picked up the faint aroma of sulphur belching from an active vent on one of the group's smaller islands. Finally, he spotted what he thought was a large cloud sitting low on the horizon. 'It was about six in the morning, and I was on the steering paddle,' he remembers. 'The boys were chatting away, saying that Nainoa thought the Kermadecs were nearby but that we may have sailed through the group at night and missed them. Well, the sun was coming up, and I had my eye on a particular cloud. I remember thinking it was a good marker to hold my course by because it wasn't moving. Then I started to have a funny feeling about it, thinking it might actually be an island.'

Shy and inexperienced, Stanley initially hesitated to call the crew's attention to his marker: 'So I watched it some more, and before long I was certain that it was an island, so I finally decided to let someone know. I grabbed Billy Richards and told him I thought I'd found the islands. He looked at me and started to smile. Nainoa was having a bit of a sleep, and Billy got him up. "Kiwi spotted the Kermadecs!"' Stanley had indeed sighted one of the group's outer islands. As the sun burnt off some lingering fog, Hōkūle'a was found to be sailing between Macauley and Curtis islands at the southern end of the chain. It was a critical sighting for Nainoa, who now knew the course to set and how far he was from their destination.

While Stanley's confidence grew out at sea, Hec filled anxious days waiting for updates of Hōkūle'a's progress by reciting karakia. 'I was very unsettled, because I knew that if anything had happened to them it would have been my fault – I would have been right in the gun for talking Nainoa into coming here in the first place.' The dragging days were worse for Stanley's parents, continues Hec: 'Niki was worrying about his son all the time. He would ring me up crying and ask, "Kei hea taku tamaiti?" Where is my son? I told him not to worry and that they weren't far away, but he was beside himself with worry the whole time Stanley was away.' When news finally came through that Hōkūle'a was within sight of land, Hec jumped in a helicopter hired by a network news crew to see her for himself. It was a memorable flight: 'Boy oh boy what a sight: such a big ocean, and Hōkūle'a was just a little speck. I'll never forget that.'

If sighting the canoe was a moment to savour for Hec, then sighting land was equally satisfying for Nainoa and the crew, as Stanley recalls: 'The evening before we reached Aotearoa we were standing around watching the sunset, and the sun started to set slightly above the horizon. We were still out of sight of land, but the way the sun was going down we could tell it was setting behind something low and flat. Nainoa knew straight away that it had to be setting behind land, and asked me where I thought we might be. I was pretty sure we were up north, maybe near my home at Te Kao.' Stanley's instincts were correct; by the following evening they had made landfall in the Bay of Islands. It was 7 December 1985. Their arrival was made all the more memorable by some forty boats and Ngātokimatawhaorua coming out to meet them. The voyage from Rarotonga had taken just sixteen days.[3]

As Hōkūle'a rested at anchor off Waitangi, respected kaumātua Sir James Henare commenced a stirring welcome for the Hawaiians:

> You have shown that it can be done, and it was done by our ancestors. To me, this is a most important occasion, and I smile and I laugh and I shall smile again tomorrow at all the critics who have said it was never done.[4]

Sir James then announced that because the Hawaiians had sailed to Aotearoa in the same manner that the ancestors of the Māori had, they were to be formally recognised as the sixth tribe of Te Tai Tokerau. The name he bestowed upon them, Ngāti Ruawāhia, had been selected by Hec in consultation with the late canon Wi Huata. It honoured the waka the Hawaiians had sailed in, as ruawāhia is the Māori name for the star Arcturus, which is called Hōkūle'a in the Hawaiian language.

It's doubtful whether even those closest to Hec truly understood the significance of Hōkūle'a's arrival in the Bay of Islands for him. Most who were there for the arrival of the canoe that early summer evening simply watched in wonder as she got closer to land, or were perhaps relieved for Niki when Stanley Conrad reached solid land. Hec, however, saw the possibility of a future that others couldn't even dream of. He had always had the gift of foresight, as some of the biggest decisions in his life illustrate; for example, the time when he forsook the safety of a foreman's job and tendered for his first bridging contract. He simply dreamed bigger than most, and had the ability and determination to see his dreams through to fruition. Like the Hawaiians before him, Hec saw a successful voyaging programme as a potential cultural rallying point for his people. When Hōkūle'a dropped anchor in the Bay of Islands he saw his future, and that future was to replicate the Hawaiian programme to the best of his ability.

As promised, when Hōkūle'a's crew returned to Hawai'i to await the settled weather of the next sailing season, Hec took charge of the canoe's well-being. The safest location for the waka, he reasoned, would be within the stone fence boundary of Te Tii Marae. Once again, Hec was able to put to use his heavy work equipment. He lifted the canoe out of the water with one of his cranes and edged the 18-metre vessel across the shoreline road to the marae, where she would rest for three months, a visual reminder to anyone who saw her of the maritime history of the Pacific.

The layover afforded Hec the opportunity to examine her at length. Her lines were pure Hawaiian, but he was able to study how she was put together, taking note, for example, of how much decking was needed to comfortably carry a dozen crew members across the ocean for weeks at a time, and how the sleeping quarters were organised above the hulls. He also examined the canoe's rigging. Māori had used sails prior to the coming of the European, but had lost the art of rigging canoes soon after they began using introduced boats for coastal sailing.

In addition to taking notes on Hōkūle'a's construction, Hec redoubled his research as his thirst for knowledge grew. He was particularly taken by passages in J H Mitchell's *Takitimu: a History of the Ngati Kahungunu People* and Elsdon Best's *The Astronomical Knowledge of the Maori*. One particular paragraph from Mitchell's book convinced him that his ancestors could not have arrived in Aotearoa by chance. It talked about the work of Tākitimu's navigators and gave the names of the stars and heavenly bodies they had used during her voyage to Aotearoa, including Atutahi (Canopus), Tautoru (Orion's Belt), Puanga (Rigel), Karewa, Takurua (Sirius), Tāwera (Venus as the morning star), Meremere (Venus as the evening star), Matariki (the Pleiades), Tama-rereti (possibly the Tail of the Scorpion), and Te Ikaroa (the Milky Way). Reading detailed accounts in such books added greatly to Hec's belief in the seafaring traditions of his ancestors. It also helped solidify his desire to build a voyaging waka of his own.

When Nainoa and his crew returned to Waitangi in late March 1986 to prepare for the next leg of their voyage, they found themselves once again at the mercy of uncooperative winds. A high-pressure system was producing north-easterlies from the precise direction the Hawaiians wished to sail, and once again there was nothing for it but to delay their departure. Hec: 'The Hawaiians really enjoyed our communal way at Te Tii Marae while they were waiting to leave for Tonga, and I tell you what, it was a sad occasion when it was finally announced that they were going to leave the following day. We had a night of speeches, and all of the crew stood up and spoke about their experience living on a marae, and each and every one of them cried before they had finished talking. It was very, very touching.'

By the end of her Voyage of Rediscovery, Hōkūle'a had sailed in excess of 11,500 nautical miles and hosted a number of individuals from various Pacific Islands. Stanley rejoined the crew for the final leg from Rangiroa in the Tuamotu Group to Hawai'i, while Hec revealed a hitherto unknown aptitude for sailing during the short three-day leg between Tonga and American Samoa. One day, with nothing but blue ocean and a distant horizon to gaze at while on the steering paddle, he noticed that the position of his shadow on the deck hardly moved during his two-hour shift: 'When the sun was out during that voyage I would watch my shadow on the deck, because I knew that if the canoe moved off course the position of my shadow would change. Of course you had to take into account the sun's movement across the sky, but it is a pretty accurate guide for short periods once you get the hang of it.' The technique was soon picked up on by the Hawaiians, and continues to be used to this day.

After the experience of hosting the Hawaiians and sailing on Hōkūle'a on the open ocean, Hec was more determined than ever to build the voyaging canoe he had been dreaming of.

Recalling the traditions of his ancestors for Nainoa Thompson had reopened the door to his past, and Hōkūle'a's arrival had shown him the door to his future. It was an exciting prospect, and, with the support of his Hawaiian mentors, one that was very achievable.

While this was an exciting period for Hec, it was also significant for Nainoa, on whom the burgeoning Hawaiian-Māori relationship wasn't lost: 'At that time Aotearoa didn't have a deep-sea voyaging canoe – but voyaging was deep within Hector, kind of sleeping, and Hōkūle'a just woke it up. Much of what he exercises in his life is very instinctual – very ancestral. I'm not able to qualify this, but I think it was just his destiny to do this kind of thing. I don't always know why connections are made, but somehow through this journey of blind relearning I ended up connecting to the right person at the right time. Ours is a relationship that has changed my life and enriched it in a way that I could never have imagined. I went back home after that first visit reinvigorated.

'I now know that the purpose of sailing Hōkūle'a to Aotearoa back then went beyond science and culture. It was about connecting people and restoring pride. In retrospect it turned out that John Rangihau was playing his cards pretty well when he didn't share everything with Hec when I first arrived. I think he knew there was going to be a relationship built, but he wanted it to be built on its own terms, without bias.'

One more important milestone in Hec's education was to come before he would begin to build his voyaging canoe however; he would finally get the opportunity to build a waka taua with his own hands.

Notes

[1] *Vaka Moana: Voyages of the Ancestors*, exhibition DVD. Auckland War Memorial Museum, 2006.

[2] Waitangi Tribunal. *Muriwhenua Fishing Report* (Wai 22, 1988), p. 255.

[3] *Honolulu Star Bulletin and Advertiser*, 9 December 1985, p. 3.

[4] Finney, B. *Voyage of Rediscovery: A Cultural Odyssey through Polynesia*. Berkeley and Los Angeles: University of California Press, 1994, p. 197.

8

THE RENAISSANCE OF THE WAKA TAUA

As the nation began to plan in earnest for the 1990 sesquicentennial of the Treaty of Waitangi, Māori set about searching for a theme that would showcase their proud history. They hoped to find a kaupapa that would be a powerful rallying point for all Māori and that would sustain a growing sense of cultural confidence and pride. From the start, Hec lobbied for that theme to be waka taua. 'Hec saw the need to inspire young Māori males in particular, and he pushed waka taua whenever he had the opportunity to address those who were making the decisions,' recalls Marty Bercic. 'He saw that we had a generation of males coming up from kōhanga reo and kura kaupapa, and the challenge was to keep them looking positively at their culture. The question was, how to keep them engaged?'

In 1989 the Maori Standing Committee of the New Zealand 1990 Commission announced that waka taua would indeed be the key focus of the Māori contribution to the celebration, and 1990 was duly dubbed the 'Year of the Waka'.

The timing was perfect as far as Hec was concerned. His business had been profitable for a number of years, and he had recently finished building what would be his final bridge. He was now in a position to invest the time and effort required to build his first waka taua. If Hec thought the stars were already beginning to align, he was pleasantly surprised when more good news arrived. Just as approval came through for him to take two trees from the Herekino State Forest for a canoe, the Government announced that substantial funding would be made available to any iwi that wanted financial assistance to construct a waka. This injection of capital meant that there would be no burden on Hec to fund the building of a canoe. 'That solved a hell of a lot of problems,' says Hec. 'The timing was just spot on, but we would have found a way to build it – there was no way I wasn't going to build a waka.'

Hec's drive had stemmed from a seemingly chance encounter with Taupuhi Eruera, a kaumātua who hailed from the small northern settlement of Utukura. Hec: 'I was at the marae at Waitangi after we relaunched Ngātokimatawhaorua back in 1974, and he could see how captivated I was by the canoe. Well, he came up to me and told me to follow him around to the back of the meeting house to a quiet spot under the shade of a tree. Once we were settled, he started to tell me all about Ngātokimatawhaorua.' Hec sat with the kaumātua for several hours, soaking in everything he had to say. He listened as Taupuhi told him about the entire construction process – from selecting logs in the forest right through to what to look out for during sea trials. 'Taupuhi was probably in his late seventies at the time and I think he died a year or two after that, but he passed on some really important information and got me really enthusiastic. Even as he was talking I was already dreaming about building a waka taua one day.'

As their kōrero began to wind up, Taupuhi went silent for a moment. Then he turned to Hec and stated that if there were any waka to be built in the north, Hec would be the one to build them: 'Nā te kaumātua rā ahau i tohi māku e tārai ngā waka o te Tai Tokerau.' He had, in effect, designated Hec as the sole individual to build waka taua in Northland.

Taupuhi had stated that the best trees for hulls are found halfway up a ridge that faces the south-west, where the rough winter weather comes from. He told Hec that as the trees mature, the side facing the cold storms grows a little slower than the sheltered side, and the heart of the tree is therefore closer to the south-western side. That side, with the heart of the tree in it, is always used for the bottom of the hull, as having the weight of the denser wood lower down added to the waka's stability. Taupuhi continued his instruction, explaining that the surest way to judge the heavy side of a tree that has already fallen is to float the log: it will automatically roll until the heavy side is at the bottom. However, there are two other ways to pick the heavy side of a tree if you don't want to go to the trouble of putting the log in water, both of which involve looking at a cross-section of the tree. The first is to visually locate the heart of the tree; if the heart is off-centre, then that is the heavy side. The second way is to find the slightly flatter side, which will be the light side.

Another piece of wisdom Taupuhi had shared with Hec was to cut trees in mid-winter, when the trees are asleep and the sap is down. Hec: 'If at all possible the idea is to drop the tree and try to have it come to rest on a slope, with the butt facing downhill to help the sap to drain out. But he warned me not to wait too long to start cutting it after it's dropped, because it's easier cutting into a tree when it's green, before it dries out and hardens. You want a little bit of juice left in it.'

Over the years Hec continued to add to his knowledge of waka, taking particular notice of the lines and dimensions of each canoe he had the opportunity to study. His notes invariably included how far along a hull the waka began to taper, and its length-to-width ratio. One example that captivated him was a waka on display at the Dargaville Museum. Fashioned from kauri, the 16-metre-long waka had been found in shifting sands on Poutō Peninsula in early 1972. According to museum staff, it was believed to have been hollowed out using fire and finished with stone tools before the arrival of Europeans.

In addition to his museum forays, Hec had also kept an ear out for leads in the communities he worked in. One tip Hec recalls concerned an old waka tīwai that he learnt about while building the bridge over the Kenana River: 'I heard a story about a kuia who had lived up the river years ago. Once a month she would ride her waka down the river on the outgoing tide, pick up her pension and buy her groceries, and then wait for the incoming tide to take her back upstream. Well, of course I was interested in seeing the waka, and I started asking if anyone knew if it was still around.' After a couple of false starts, Hec managed to track it down to a farm shed, and organised permission to view it. 'So I jumped in my truck after work one evening and headed out to have a look. When my eyes adjusted to the light in the shed,

I realised I'd actually seen the waka years before, when it was sitting at the back of Kenana Marae. It wasn't in the best shape, but you could still tell that it had nice lines, and I was pretty excited to see it again.'

Hec carefully measured the decaying waka; he was so taken by it that he decided to build a replica. 'When we tried it out it was fantastic. You could just push it out into the river, sit down and it went on its own. You didn't even have to use a paddle to steer it. You could just lean to one side and it would come around.'

It was undoubtedly the combination of Taupuhi's teachings and his own experience looking after Ngātokimatawhaorua that had most influenced Hec when it came time to build his own waka. 'When I started planning to build my first waka taua I decided that I wanted to do everything as our tūpuna would have, especially when it came to the spiritual side of things. I quickly realised though that nobody here in the north had any experience with the particular karakia I needed, so that became my first assignment – to find and learn those karakia.'

Hec was also determined to make sure that appropriate protocols were followed in other aspects of the build, which included banning women from the construction site. He arranged for a pair of hand-painted signs saying as much to be hung outside the carving shed, to ensure everyone was aware of the site's tikanga. When asked about this at the time, Hec explained that women had never been allowed near waka taua work sites in the old days, and that it was a custom that he wanted to respect: 'I figured that if we couldn't stick to the traditions that I was learning about, we might as well not build the canoe at all.'

As Hec finalised preparations for the felling of the two trees he'd been allocated, one of his closest supporters, Sir James Henare, passed away unexpectedly. 'Sir James was very well respected, and hundreds of people attended his funeral. When it came my turn to stand and pay my respects, I started by saying, "Our big tōtara has fallen, so tomorrow I am going to the forest, to Tāne's domain, and I am going to cut down the trees for a waka taua."' It was, Hec would later confess, a calculated move; he knew full well that there could be no turning back once he had delivered his speech.

'When we arrived at the Herekino State Forest the next morning we performed the waharoa karakia to ask permission to enter into Tāne's domain and to let him know why we were taking his tree. Then we drove about 10 kilometres into the forest, along one of the old logging roads, stopping at a spot near the two kauri we had been allocated, and we walked in from there. To be honest, they weren't the best trees. One was okay, but the other was dead – still standing, but dead. What we thought didn't really matter though; they were the ones the Department of Conservation had put aside for us, so we had to use them.'

The group performed more karakia once they arrived at the trees, and then started a small fire using wood chips from the first cuts. According to tradition, the ascending smoke links Tāne, guardian of the forest, to his father Rangi-nui – the Sky Father. A second fire then cooked a small amount of food for the workmen. Hec: 'In the olden days they would give workers special food harvested from both the sea and from the land. The workers would have a mouthful, and the remains of the kai would be placed at the base of the tree and then covered over with foliage so that the birds couldn't get at it. Then, once those two parts of the ceremony were completed, the tree could be taken.'

Any apprehension Hec may have had when it came time to fell the trees was allayed when his elder brother Hugh, a forestry veteran of thirty years and a bush boss for the Kaitāia Timber Company, took control of proceedings. Hec: 'Hugh knew what he was doing, and everything went smoothly. He started by studying the head of each tree to work out which way they should fall, and then he got to work.' Despite Hec's matter-of-fact attitude towards such things, when he looks back on cutting down those first two trees he still gets a tingle down his spine: 'The whole ceremony was quite an emotional time for all of us, of course, what with Sir James lying in state. And when the birds stopped singing after the first tree had fallen, it was like they were giving a minute's silence. It was quite beautiful really.'

When it came to deciding on the length and hull proportions for his new waka, Hec once again fell back on the knowledge Taupuhi had passed on to him. The kaumātua had touched on the need to take into consideration a tree's height-to-breadth ratio, a subject that Hec later spent considerable time thinking about: 'A tree's diameter has a direct influence on the final length of the waka: you can make a waka as long as you like, but the rule of thumb is the longer it is, the wider it needs to be. If a long canoe is too narrow, there's a hell of a strain on the hull. The minimum width of tree I'll work with is 4 feet [1.2 metres], although I prefer to work with logs around 6 feet [1.82 metres] across. A log 6 feet across will allow me to build a waka around the 60–70-foot [16–21-metre] mark with a 5½- to 6-foot [1.6–1.8-metre] beam. That's the ideal as far as I'm concerned.'

Another detail Taupuhi had instructed Hec to keep in mind was to ensure the bottom of the hull was of a reasonable thickness. A solid keel is necessary to keep the waka from twisting and warping along its length, and the weight along the bottom helps to keep the waka stable in the water. To illustrate the point, the 35.7-metre-long Ngātokimatawhaorua is 300 millimetres thick at the bottom of her hull; several waka built by Hec in recent years that sit in the 15- to 16.5-metre-long range have hulls around 150 millimetres thick.

The reality is that if you know your ratios, constructing a waka taua isn't particularly challenging. In fact, it could be likened to assembling a giant kit-set toy, albeit one weighing several tonnes. That said, you do have to know wood: both its strengths and weaknesses and how to work it. And, critically, you have to know how the various components fit together. The hull of Hec's first waka was built from two logs: the centre section of the waka was fashioned from a single log, and the stern and the bow came from the second tree. Hec recalls that he was painstakingly careful to conserve as much wood as he could while hollowing out the hull: 'In the old days they burnt out the inside of the hull, but I had to try to save as much timber as I could for the other parts, like the rauawa, tauihu and paepae. I didn't want to waste any of it. We worked out our cuts, and carefully sliced as much as we could off the top of the log.'

While his carving crew started shaping the two rauawa, Hec began working on the haumi joins where the three sections of the hull are joined. As Hec explains, haumi joins are virtually self-locking: 'I made a point of going to the haumi joins on Ngātokimatawhaorua whenever we met swells so I could judge how good the design was, and I'd say that the haumi join is without equal for the job required, especially when the paepae that covers the horizontal join between the rauawa and the side walls of the hull is lashed in place.'

With the three sections of the hull lashed together, Hec began to work on the interior of the hull. 'Back in pre-European days there was virtually an unlimited supply of trees fit for constructing waka, so, as I understand it, our tūpuna would try to use suitable trees growing close to water where possible. The reason for that, other than for ease of launching, was that waka builders often used water to judge the straightness of the canoe's inside lines.' It was considered, Hec says, a near foolproof method to keep the inside walls of the hull straight: 'If you half-fill the hull with water and then look along the edges where the water meets the wood, you can actually see where it isn't straight, mark the spot, and chip away.' Through sheer luck, Hec fell upon a similar method. By happenstance his hull was sitting north–south when he began working on it, and he was able to use the shadow cast by the rising sun on one side of the hull and the shadow cast by the setting sun on the other to judge the straightness of the inside of the hull.

With the hull nearing completion, work was begun on two of the most intricately carved components of the waka: the taurapa and tauihu. Hec remembers Taupuhi telling him that the more taniwha there are on a tauihu, the more mana it carries. The tauihu Hec replicates for most of his prows has four taniwha on its extremities and another six incorporated within the inner design detail. The spiral work that appears within tauihu is no less intricate; according to Hec, it represents whirlpools and upwells such as Te Korokoro-o-te-Parata, an upwell that is remembered as having nearly claimed the migration waka Aotea. According to tradition, Te Korokoro-o-te-Parata is located in a part of the ocean near the Kermadec group known as Tautope-ki-te-uru.

Sitting below the tauihu at the very front of the waka is a figure representing Tūmatauenga – the god of war. 'He's there to let Tangaroa know that Tāne is in his domain,' explains Hec, 'and further down, the puhoro design under the waka is likened to the weave on top of a korowai. The tauihu is the head of the waka and the puhoro covers the shoulders.'

The taurapa also has its own story. According to Taupuhi the figure carved into the top of the sternpost represents the ancestor Puhi-Kai-Ariki, and from that figure two ribs descend: one representing the taha wairua, which comes from the figure's mouth, and the other the taha tangata, which runs down from the figure's neck. The figure that sits at the base of the taurapa facing forward is usually named after an important ancestor, and the stylised figure directly behind the ancestral figure is Puhi-Moana-Ariki. All of the figures connect up with the kaitiaki carved into the two rauawa that run the length of the waka to the tauihu sitting at the front of the canoe.

While Hec has always had a deep respect for the skills of his ancestors, duplicating artefacts such as Ngātokimatawhaorua's tauihu (which was originally copied from a prow residing in the British Museum) has given him a far greater appreciation of the ability of early carvers: 'The old-time carvers were fantastic craftsmen who really understood wood, how to prepare it and how to work with it, and it's not until you try to replicate their work that you really understand the level of their skill. The original of the tauihu we base our replicas on is in England and remains in great condition after maybe 200 years, yet we've always had trouble with our wood cracking. In the end I had to turn to lamination to duplicate their work.'

With the canoe's construction running to schedule, Hec travelled to the Bay of Plenty with a small delegation in mid-1989 for discussions relating to her naming: 'We went down to ask Ngāti Awa if we could use the name Mataatua. It's an ancestral name that has strong connections to both Northland and the Bay of Plenty, and we didn't want to use the name without consulting them. Some of our kaumātua from Whangaroa had already started talking with the elders from down Whakatāne about our shared history, so it was the right thing to do.' According to traditions, soon after the Mataatua people migrated to Aotearoa, Puhi, the younger brother of Mataatua's captain Toroa, decided to strike out on his own. Departing with a small following, he sailed the Mataatua waka north in the hope of finding land to establish himself on. He finally found suitable land in the vicinity of the Tākou River, just south of Matauri Bay on Northland's east coast. By the late twentieth century the two branches of the Mataatua people had for all intents and purposes been separated for hundreds of years.

The delegation was warmly received at Te Teko where Ngāti Awa listened to Hec's proposal. His request, however, caused no small amount of consternation; Ngāti Awa were themselves building a waka taua for the celebrations, and had also planned to name their waka Mataatua. It put them in a difficult position, but they did acknowledge that their northern relations had a claim to the name as well. Eventually a compromise was found: Ngāti Awa would name their waka Mataatua-Toi, leaving Hec free to name his waka Mataatua-Puhi. It was a thoughtful concession, which allowed the two sections of Mataatua to continue working towards a stronger relationship.

As the hui wound up, Ngāti Awa kaumātua approached Hec and asked him if he would consider setting up a training programme for their paddlers. They realised that there would be precious little time to train their crew between the launch of Mataatua-Toi and their expected arrival at Waitangi, and they needed expert help. Hec, ever keen to foster waka culture wherever he could, readily agreed to their request, and it wasn't long before vanloads of eager paddlers began to make the ten-hour trip north to Hec's for weekend wānanga. Mataatua-Toi kaihoe and future Te Aurere navigator Jack Thatcher recalls the arrangement: 'Hec had a kaihoe programme that had been going since the Ngātokimatawhaorua's re-launch, so in terms of training, they were a great help to us. The other really cool thing that came out of our trips north was that the crews got together and things started to click between the northern end and the southern end. The sharing of knowledge was a brilliant stroke because it brought everyone together. I remember one of our kaumātua, Ben Mamaku I think it was, talking with us about the canoes bringing Mataatua together – how in the old days we had one waka and two people, and that now it was more like we had two waka and one people.'

It was a sentiment echoed by Te Rarawa kaumātua Simon Snowden at Mataatua-Puhi's official launch: 'It's a very important day for us. The linking of the two people of the Mataatua here in the north and in Whakatane, and the linking of the kaumātua with the rangatahi.'[1] The canoe, Snowden continued, linked them not only with their past, but also with their future.

In an echo of Ngātokimatawhaorua's launch in 1939, Mataatua-Puhi's big day didn't proceed quite as smoothly as hoped. Like their forebears fifty-one years earlier, those charged with manhandling the waka into the water had difficulty moving the canoe from her resting place. One of their number noted that when the first efforts had been made to move the canoe it had been heavy and unwieldy; 'But then we heard the kaumatua start their karakia and you could feel it giving you strength.'[2] With muscles straining and backs bent, the men soon had the sleek waka moving towards the river. Once afloat, she looked every inch the waka taua Hec had dreamed of. It was several minutes before the din from the excited spectators had died down enough for Hec to recite the karakia and officially name the waka Mataatua-Puhi. Then, with the formalities complete, the command was given, and the crew began to paddle the waka along Awapoko River to enthusiastic applause. It was a significant moment for Hec, and indeed for the revival of waka culture in the north.

In a matter of months Hec had built his first waka taua, and had fulfilled not only his own dreams, but also Taupuhi's prophecy:

'Nā te kaumātua rā ahau i tohi māku e tārai ngā waka o te Tai Tokerau.' He would later admit that he couldn't help the tears running down his face when the waka was finally on the river.

In the wider context, Hec could already see that the renaissance of waka taua would be significant for the widespread community involvement it fostered. In time the reappearance of waka in northern waters would see many, many hundreds of Māori respond to the kaupapa. Some became kaihoe on the waka, while others learnt to build waka or dedicated themselves to related subjects, such as studying waka history or traditions. This was, above all, what Hec had hoped for when he had joined those lobbying for the relaunching of Ngātokimatawhaorua more than two and a half decades earlier.

The success of Mataatua-Puhi, both on the water and within the Māori community, encouraged Hec to embark on a career that would eventually see him build or oversee the construction of more than thirty waka. What's more, his dedication to the kaupapa would see him play a leading role in the resurgence of waka culture across the nation.

Extremely knowledgeable, but humble with it, Hec was the perfect man to play a leading role in the revival. But first, he had to oversee the coming together of twenty-two waka at Waitangi.

Notes

[1] *Northern Advocate*, 22 November 1989, p. 12.

[2] Ibid.

Ngātokimatawhaorua on the water off Waitangi, 6 February 1974. The relaunch of the war canoe would have a profound effect on Hec and lead to a long involvement with waka. Hec would eventually become the guardian of the waka taua.
Photo supplied by Busby family

Ngātokimatawhaorua being brought ashore with the help of one of Hec's winch-carrying trucks, c 1975.
Photo supplied by Busby family

Hec lending a hand to carve a maihi for Ngātokimatawhaorua's new canoe shed, Te Korowai o Maikuku, on the shore at Hobson Beach, under the watchful eye of Dan Whiu, 1974 or 1975.
Photo supplied by Busby family

Prince Charles and Lady Diana ride in Ngātokimatawhaorua in the Bay of Islands, 1983. Hec stands behind Prince Charles, while Hilda sits in front of the royal couple.

Photo supplied by Busby family

Workmen cut a scarf in one of the giant kauri trees used for the hull of Mataatua-Puhi in 1989. Hec's older brother Hugh, a long-time forestry worker, oversaw the operation in Herekino State Forest and ensured that every care was taken in felling the trees.
Photo supplied by Busby family

A huge section of kauri, felled for Hec's first waka, Mataatua-Puhi, being transported on the back of one of Hec's trucks. Hec's access to heavy equipment from his business would prove pivotal in the success of his waka programme.
Photo supplied by Busby family

Hec shaping the hull of Mataatua-Puhi at his Doubtless Bay property, late 1989.
Photo copyright Arno Gasteiger

Hilda (front left) leading her performing rōpū to the stage at Waitangi, c 1990.
Photo supplied by Busby family

Hec standing alongside a dendroglyph on the Chatham Islands. Carved into kopi (karaka) trees, the figures represent ancestors, fish, trees, birds, weapons and tools.

Photo supplied by Busby family

A cloaked Hec performs a whaikōrero outside the Kerikeri stone store. In his later years Hec has become a respected kaumātua, representing his people with distinction on many fronts.
Photo supplied by Busby family

9

FROM THE HEART OF A NATION TO FOREIGN LANDS

Mataatua-Puhi having been launched, Hec was now free to concentrate on preparing for the upcoming celebrations to mark the 150th anniversary of the signing of the Treaty of Waitangi. Not only was he overseeing Mataatua-Puhi and Ngātokimatawhaorua on the day; he was also responsible for hosting the twenty other waka that would be descending on the Bay of Islands from across the nation. The majority of the waka on their way north had been constructed especially for the celebration, and these canoes were at the forefront of a mini-renaissance. Many craftsmen involved in the projects had revived skills that had lain dormant for generations; others had been forced to adapt their existing carving and woodworking knowledge. Many of the waka were built with native woods, and either shaped from solid tree trunks or constructed using lamination processes. A handful of iwi had decided on fibreglass hulls, and the single vessel representing the Chatham Islands was made in the traditional manner from bundles of cut and dried raupō lashed to a wooden frame.

In addition to housing and feeding the waka crews, Hec and Hilda were heavily involved in preparations for the national kapa haka competition that was also being staged at Waitangi that year. The couple had become well versed in organising large events; when Whāngārei had successfully hosted the festival two years earlier, in 1988, both had been central figures in its success. Pita Paraone was among those who witnessed them in action first-hand: 'That was when I saw Hector at his peak. He was able to take the national competition to a level that had never been seen before. Once again, through Hector's style of management, the support of Hilda and the backing of the committee, the festival was able to achieve a profit.' Paraone continues: 'Hec is a man who once he sets his mind to a task will make sure that it gets done, and he also ensures that there is a quality of achievement in terms of the tasks that have been set. Ultimately I believe that the success of the 1988 festival contributed to government deciding that the 1990 kapa haka festival should also be held in Te Tai Tokerau: this time at Waitangi under a big top.'

Having been central to the organisation of nearly twenty Waitangi Day events, Hec and Hilda had more than enough experience to oversee preparations for the 1990 festival. They knew what they were about, and didn't get side-tracked by any peripheral issues: a fact that several government ministers appreciated over the years. Don McKinnon (later Sir Don), the minister responsible for the Waitangi Day commemorations, developed a close working relationship with both Hec and Hilda:

> I got to know them quite well, because we went up there for a number of weekends in advance of the day and they were at all of the meetings. Hilda was always solidly behind Hec, who was a genial, friendly sort of a guy who was always ready with a laugh or two. I remember he was easy to get along with and I had an immediate empathy with him. He was always solid, dependable and there were never any antics. And I know he didn't have any truck for people interrupting our meetings. A couple of times Hone Harawira came in when we were in Te Tii meeting house and tried to disrupt the whole thing, and Hec would just sit him down. It was a 'Listen boy – sit there and you can speak when you are spoken to' sort of situation.
>
> Over the years I've met quite a few people who know Hec and they all said he is totally dependable. If he says he is going to finish the bridge on the fourteenth, then he'd finish it on the fourteenth, even if he has to round up additional workers to make sure he does. With any organisation it is the Hec Busbys that hold everything together. They are dependable: straight up and down and they get things done. They are the natural leaders, and you can quickly tell them apart.

With Waitangi Day looming and Hec busy finalising arrangements for the visiting waka, the decision had to be made whether to truck Mataatua-Puhi to Waitangi or paddle her. Either way, Hec would have to travel down early so that he could be there before any of the visiting waka arrived. In the end, Hec decided that Mataatua-Puhi would go by sea, reasoning that the 55-mile paddle south along the coast would be a good trial for the waka and allow the crew an extended period to familiarise themselves with the vessel's personality.

By coincidence the canoe followed the route that the famed ancestor Tamatea Pōkai Whenua had taken centuries before. In another twist of fate, Hec's crew encountered similar sea conditions to those Tamatea's crew had endured once they left the shelter of Doubtless Bay. Hec explains: 'Tamatea Pōkai Whenua was a very mischievous man, and at one point when he was on the run from one husband or another he decided that he had better leave the north once and for all. So he gathered a crew and launched his canoe from Aurere Beach – just along from where my house is now. When they got out from Doubtless Bay, near Nuku-taurua rock, the wind changed and the sea started to get up. Some of his paddlers got scared, and an anguished call came: "Eh, Kauri e. Ka mate tātou!" "Hey Kauri" – that was one of Tamatea Pōkai Whenua's names – "we will all die out here!" That's when he replied with what has become a well-known whakatauākī: "He rāngai maomao, ka taka ki tua o Nuku-taurua e kore a muri e hokia." A shoal of maomao that passes beyond Nuku-taurua rock never returns. He knew what was waiting behind him and that he would be killed, so he wasn't keen to turn back.'

As in the tradition, when Hec's waka Mataatua-Puhi reached Nuku-taurua rock, growing seas began to make it difficult for the crew to control the vessel. Unlike Tamatea Pōkai Whenua, however, Hec did have the option to return to land. When they reached shore, he ordered all but a core group of experienced paddlers to disembark. Those asked to stay on board would help steer the waka while it was towed south. Hec: 'In the end the trip to Waitangi took two days because of the delay caused by the change in plans. We arrived at the entrance to Whangaroa Harbour just as dark began to descend at the end of the first day, and we slept the night at one of the local marae.'

The conditions were no easier the following morning, with rolling swells and fresh winds buffeting the canoe all the way to Waitangi. Hec's crew had been out in perhaps some of the roughest seas a modern-day waka taua had faced. True to form, Hec focused on the canoe's performance rather than the conditions, taking great confidence from his vessel's seaworthiness: 'Oh, I was thrilled. The waka had taken everything thrown at her and proven herself in testing conditions. That voyage alone showed me that everything Taupuhi had told me about building waka was spot on. I wouldn't say it was a relief to see how she went, because I had a fair idea she was fine after watching her when she was launched, but she felt stable on the rough water, so I was very happy.'

When Waitangi Day dawned, a flotilla of twenty-two waka was lined up along the shoreline. Most of the kaihoe and their elders had spent the night with their waka, reciting karakia and chanting, while offshore a strong navy presence swayed at anchor.

Like it had for the 1940 centennial celebrations, the day started with a re-enactment of the signing of the Treaty of Waitangi. This was followed by Ngātokimatawhaorua receiving a salute from the crew of HMNZS *Canterbury*. Among the canoe's crew sat broadcaster Haare Williams. 'It was an incredible experience to be on Ngātokimatawhaorua at that time,' he recalls: 'When we approached the *Canterbury* the officers and crew were lined up along the deck, and as we came alongside there was a whistle and they all saluted. The kaihoe returned the salute by thumping their paddles in time upon the waka as they glided along the length of the ship. When we got to the other end a second blow of the whistle finished their salute, their tribute, and the kaihoe started paddling to their chant – tōkihi, tōkihi. Wow, what a moving moment.'

Once again, as she had sixteen years previously, Ngātokimatawhaorua had the honour of escorting Queen Elizabeth II and her husband the Duke of Edinburgh to shore, but this time they were supported by an impressive flotilla of waka representing many iwi from across the nation. It must surely have been a proud day for all involved; none more so than those who had chosen waka as the focal point for the Māori contribution to the day. Thousands of Māori had been involved in the building and manning of the canoes, and hundreds of thousands of New Zealanders were captivated by the sight of the waka, either in person or on television, being paddled across the waters of the Bay of Islands.

A few days after the event Hec received a letter from the Government expressing the greatful thanks of Her Majesty. In part the communiqué read, 'The proud Waitangi craft which provided the close escort for the Queen's Barge stood out … and Her Majesty has asked me to write to congratulate you on organising such a splendid and moving spectacle.' The letter concluded by acknowledging that 'the project aroused enormous enthusiasm throughout Māoridom' and offered

Her Majesty's 'warmest congratulations to you and all who took part'.

While Ngātokimatawhaorua, Matatua-Puhi and the other waka were headlining at Waitangi, an ocean away the Polynesian Voyaging Society was busy trying to locate suitable logs to build a second voyaging canoe. They had searched their own koa forests for nine months and had failed to find a solitary tree big and healthy enough to build even a single hull for a voyaging canoe. With their own resources exhausted, they turned to the origin of drift logs that occasionally washed up on their shores: the Pacific Northwest of America. Nainoa: 'There was a second source of trees that the early Hawaiians used. In fact Captain Vancouver recorded in his ship's log that he had seen a 60-foot-long canoe that was made out of the finest pine, on the island of Kaua'i. Well he knew pine wasn't native to Hawai'i, so he questioned the chiefs and they told him that it had been found on the beach. It was, they said, a gift from the gods.'

Calling on their contacts, the Hawaiians organised an introduction to Byron Mallott, then the CEO of Sealaska, an Alaskan corporation charged with providing economic, cultural and social benefits for its native shareholders. Mallott, a Tlingit himself, agreed to contribute the needed logs on three conditions: the Hawaiians were never to ask how much the logs were worth; they were never to return the logs; and, lastly, they had to inspect the trees to make sure that they met their exact specifications before they would be cut down. 'They explained to us that their survival in Alaska over thousands of years depended on their relationship to the resources they have, so the trees had to be 100 per cent right before they would cut them down,' recalls Nainoa. 'From that I clearly understood from the very beginning that these were a deeply spiritual people. We don't have that depth in Hawai'i now. Our ancestors had it, but we're disconnected. I knew Hector had that depth though. I've been in the kauri forests with him and I remember him saying that they are the domain of his ancestors, so being with him was a very important learning process for us. If we were ever going to build a voyaging canoe with trees from our own forests we were going to have to make that connection with our ancestors, and to do that we would need to know the spiritual and cultural side of things – so Hector became very important to us.'

Once the trees had been identified and an agreement formalised, Hec and representatives from the Polynesian Voyaging Society flew to Shelikof Island, Alaska, where suitable spruce trees had been identified. For Hec, the trip was an opportunity to return the support the Hawaiians had given him: 'I was happy to go to Alaska to help out, but as soon as I got into their forest I felt a little uncomfortable, out of place. Their forests aren't like ours: you don't hear any birds at all, and that stung me straight away.' Even though he had been flown to Alaska specifically to participate in the ceremony, Hec felt uncomfortable, and he approached Nainoa to share his feelings. Nainoa was sympathetic, but reiterated that he wanted Hec to participate, and that they needed him to help bridge the gap between themselves and the Alaskans. 'I agreed to do my part reluctantly,' recalls Hec, 'and I told him that I didn't want to take over the whole thing. Something on the inside was telling me not to.'

After the ceremony, Hec was able to spend some time with their hosts. Nainoa: 'Out of all of us, Hec was the one who connected the best with the Alaskan elders. I distinctly remember that he quickly clicked into the conversations of the world of the elders – much more so than I would have been able to do. They had an extraordinary connection, storytelling and exchanges and so forth. They spoke a very deep native language, and by native I mean native to the land. It's a language that goes deeper than words. That was very impressive to me.'

When Hec arrived back home, he began to put his plans into action. The time he had spent in Nainoa's company had given him the confidence to build his own voyaging canoe, and critically he knew that Nainoa and his friends could provide the specialised support that he would need. It would be an audacious undertaking given Hec's relative inexperience, but he was ready. In truth, Hec had come a long way from the nervous passenger who had sailed on Hōkūle'a from the Big Island to Miloli'i just three and a half years earlier. With the ever-present support of Hilda, he was about to commence his own journey into the world of his seafaring ancestors.

10

TE AURERE

While Hec's desire to build a voyaging canoe had been growing ever since Hōkūle'a had sailed into the Bay of Islands in 1985, he didn't make his plans public until he had approached the Te Rarawa tribal council seeking support for his project in early 1990. His proposal was to build a double-hulled voyaging canoe capable of sailing to Rarotonga for the 1992 Festival of Pacific Arts. While it was an ambitious undertaking, it was one Hec was confident he could accomplish. He had already built a waka taua to exacting standards and launched her to great acclaim, and he could count on the support of Nainoa and several other members of the Polynesian Voyaging Society to guide him in the more technical aspects of the project. Most importantly, he had the self-belief and determination needed to build a canoe capable of following in the wake of his revered ancestor, Tūmoana. Hec: 'I knew that Tūmoana had sailed back to his Pacific Island homeland after voyaging here, and that is what I wanted to do – to sail into the Pacific from Aotearoa. I knew within me that I had the experience to take the project on at that time. I'd looked after Ngātokimatawhaorua for some fifteen years by then, and had already finished Mataatua-Puhi before I started thinking really seriously about building a voyaging canoe.'

Disappointingly, Hec encountered barriers from the outset. None of the council members had deep-water sailing experience and, at least in Hec's eyes, they were overly cautious in dealing with his request. Robert Gable: 'I don't think the committee were intentionally obstructive, but there is a well-known saying in Māori circles: if you don't want something to happen, have a hui. The modern way on the marae is to consult with everybody, and it doesn't always work if you want to get something done quickly – and of course Hector wasn't going to sit around. He wanted to get on with it.'

With the festival imminent, Hec found the committee's procrastination particularly annoying, and he finally decided to bypass them altogether and push on with the project under his own steam. While Hec understood that the committee's assistance would be beneficial when it came to requesting suitable trees to build his vessel, he reasoned that its absence wouldn't prove insurmountable. He had already received encouraging personal support from two senior Te Rarawa kaumātua, Simon Snowden and Graham Latimer (later Sir Graham), both of whom held considerable mana in the north. What's more, he also had the backing of the influential Te Tai Tokerau District Māori Council, so he was somewhat bewildered when his application to fell two kauri trees was declined by the Department of Conservation. On the verge of seeing his dream dashed at the first hurdle, Hec took the extreme measure of ringing then Prime Minister Jenny Shipley to plead his case directly; remarkably, official approval for the kauri arrived less than two weeks later. Any feelings of relief Hec felt after securing the trees were tempered somewhat when he eventually got to view them: 'One tree was fine, but the other tree tapered very quickly, and I could tell right away that I would have trouble when it came to shaping matching hulls. But that was what I was given to work with, so that was that.'

Among those invited to the Herekino State Forest to witness the felling of the trees was an old acquaintance of Hec's, Haare Williams. 'As always, being in Hec's presence was a wonderful experience. There were a number of kaumātua there on the day: Simon Snowden, Graham Latimer, Marlin Epiha and others, and a number of youths were present as well. Hec's brother Hugh supervised the cutting of the trees, which only took a few minutes, and there was complete silence in the forest when the trees hit the ground. Not a single bird could be heard for what seemed like several minutes. Soon after Hec had completed the appropriate karakia we returned to his home for a feast near the site he planned to build the waka.'

Once again, Hec's property would prove to be the perfect location for a work site. Its isolation at the southern end of Tokerau Beach on a thumb of land between the ocean and Awapoko River meant that Hec didn't often receive uninvited visitors, and he was able to erect a barrier across his road without inconveniencing neighbours. 'I had decided early on that I wanted to stick to the same protocols we had observed when we built Mataatua-puhi, so we put the barrier up to warn people about the tapu work we were doing.'

As word of the project spread, three more respected kaumātua added their voices of support to those of Snowden and Latimer. Reverend Wi Huata, who had been a padre of the 28th Māori Battalion in World War Two; Rua Cooper, one of the Māori Queen's spokesmen from Tainui; and John Rangihau, who had introduced Nainoa to Hec, all offered their unwavering support over the coming months. Hec: 'After we got the logs back to my property, those three kaumātua travelled up regularly to visit, and inevitably they'd refer to the logs as "our" taonga, theirs as well as ours. Those were thrilling words, and they rung in my ears – Tā tātou taonga e takoto mai nā – Our treasure that lies there. When I heard that kind of talk coming from people outside my tribe, it really made me strong. They were basically saying I was representing all Māori, and in the end that's why I opened crew selection up to people from right throughout the land.'

While Hec had been able to study existing waka taua when he was building Mataatua-Puhi, there were no surviving Māori voyaging canoes on which to base the design of his new double-hulled waka. Instead he made do with the freshly minted plans for the Hawaiian canoe being built with the logs felled in Alaska. Nainoa: 'We gave him the preliminary designs for Hawai'iloa, but, to be honest, I think we actually did Hector a disservice. The design hadn't yet been refined, but fortunately he was smart enough to recognise that our plans had flaws. He looked at our design, understood it, and then made the adjustments needed. Once again it goes back to his instincts, which I really think are ancestral. He is a very, very smart man.'

Hec added a few Māori finishes to the waka when he adapted the original plans, such as scalloping on the outer surface of the hulls and carvings copied from two ancient artefacts, a tauihu and taurapa, which had been found in swampland near his home. 'They were housed at the Auckland War Memorial Museum but weren't on display at the time we visited, so the curator took us into a back room to view them. When I first approached them I had to avert my eyes. I didn't realise they were going to affect me like that, and it took a few minutes until I could compose myself and mihi to them. It was very emotional seeing them in person, and I had to think long and hard about whether it was right to copy them for my waka. In the end I decided that it was okay, and they have looked after the canoe ever since.'

As well as providing the Hawai'iloa design plans, the Polynesian Voyaging Society donated US$5,000 towards Hec's waka – a not unsubstantial amount at the time. Nainoa later said of the donation: 'It was one avenue that we were able to show our support for Hector, but the donation was tremendously outweighed by what Hector had given us. It's very hard to quantify his contribution to our own growth, because it's not just about him helping us out with a karakia or hosting us when we travel to New Zealand: it was really about allowing us to grow, and he really nurtured our growth. The donation was basically symbolic compared to what he gave us.'

With the two kauri trees lying at Aurere, Hec got to work shaping the hulls, while his team of workers began the long process of crafting and carving the cross-beams that would connect the two hulls, along with the mast and boom and the three large steering paddles. The tauihu and taurapa Hec had viewed at the Auckland War Memorial Museum were also faithfully reproduced, thanks to photographs and video footage taken during the visit.

Although the canoe's construction progressed to schedule, the project was very nearly permanently derailed by a fishing accident that occurred during one of Hec's solo forays into Doubtless Bay. It was 25 September 1990. 'I was fishing a favourite spot about three kilometres out from home and for some reason I couldn't get my anchor to set, and on top of that, I was having trouble starting the outboard motor. In my frustration I got a bit careless and pushed the choke in just as I was sitting down. Well, of course the motor finally burst into life, the boat jumped forward and I was flipped off the back.' By the time Hec had surfaced and regathered his thoughts, the boat was already out of reach, motoring in ever-widening circles.

Alone and too far from shore to contemplate swimming back, Hec realised that his only chance of survival was if one of the local fishermen caught sight of him or his boat when they returned from distant fishing grounds in the evening. 'When I knew I wasn't going to get back to my boat I kicked off my gumboots and coat and said a simple karakia, asking that I be spared because I had a job to do – I wanted to finish Te Aurere. At first I thought I'd be okay, but after I had been in the sea for about an hour I started to swallow a bit of water, and that's when I began to have doubts. There wasn't much I could do, so I said a final karakia, rolled onto my back and waited for the end. I actually relived my whole life during that period. I started thinking about growing up, who owed me money and who I owed money to, about my land, my business and all that. I really thought it was the end. Then, out of nowhere, I felt something shaking my right shoulder. I opened my eyes and looked to my right, but there was nothing there. I couldn't quite work it out, but for some reason I rolled over to my left side and I saw it: a fishing boat coming to rescue me.'

Noel Hartley had been returning from setting long lines when he came across Hec's boat, drifting in the bay. His immediate instinct was to motor upwind of the boat's position and scan the ocean's surface for her crew. He eventually caught sight of an exhausted Hec and, after quite a struggle, managed to haul him to safety aboard his boat. Hec, already suffering from the onset of hypothermia, had been in the water just short of an hour and a half. Hec recognised that he was remarkably lucky to have survived.

Once he had recovered from his ordeal, Hec passed the closing months of 1990 and most of 1991 working on his waka, save for intermittent periods carving pou for marae and completing a few other small commissions. By late 1991 the waka was for all intents and purposes finished.

The Māori Queen, Te Atairangikaahu, and her entourage were among those to witness the launch, along with a strong contingent from Hawai'i, headed by Pinky Thompson. Also prominent among the excited crowd was Simon Snowden, one of only two kaumātua remaining from the group of elders who had encouraged Hec during the waka's construction; John Rangihau had passed on, as had Wi Huata and Rua Cooper.

The launch was the last of several emotional ceremonies the Hawaiian group attended while in the north. Earlier in the week they had formally acknowledged their place as the sixth tribe of Te Tai Tokerau by presenting a 2.7-metre-tall ki'i (tiki or pou) crafted from ohi'a hardwood to their hosts. The ki'i, representing Māui-pā-mamao – Māui who touches the farthest extremities – was set alongside Māori pou at Waitangi. There had also been a number of school and marae visits.

But the day of the launch of Hec's waka hourua was different. Pinky understood that this event had the potential to influence the future for an entire people. Māori had been set apart; here was a means to reconnect them to their long-separated Polynesian roots. It was with no small measure of delight then that Pinky Thompson watched the canoe being trucked past blossoming pōhutukawa trees down to the beach below Hec's home, where it was carefully lowered onto the beach.

With the canoe sitting patiently, waiting for the waters of Doubtless Bay to embrace her, Hec announced that breakfast was ready, and soon many of the assembled well-wishers filed back over the low sandhills for a warm meal. A handful of individuals stayed with the waka, however, including Jack Thatcher. 'To be honest I was just sort of buzzing out and didn't feel like eating, so me and a mate stayed behind to take it all in. We'd been standing there, gazing at the waka for perhaps twenty minutes, when the weather started to change, and before we knew it the waka was being picked up by the waves and dropped onto the beach.'

Nainoa, keeping a watchful eye on the canoe from the house, immediately recognised the danger, and returned to the beach where he called for volunteers to carry the canoe's anchors out into the bay. Jack: 'Up goes my hand, and before I knew it four or five of us were carrying anchors out through the surf, with waves coming over our heads and all. We got the first anchor out as far as we could, and secured it to the seabed, and then we returned to the waka and started to pull her out through the breakers. Once we got her out past the first row we jumped into the water again to carry the second anchor a bit further out. In effect we were manhandling one anchor out while the other was keeping the waka from being pushed back to shore.' By the time the waka was safely out past the breakers, Hec and most of the crowd had returned to the beach.

With the waka now afloat within Tangaroa's domain, Hec recited the appropriate karakia and formally named his 17-metre long waka Te Aurere. The name, so familiar to many now, was in fact a last-minute substitution; Hec had been persuaded by a close relative to drop his preferred name of Māmaru in the days leading up to the ceremony. 'I'd chosen Māmaru because it was the name of an ancestral waka from the north and of course I wanted to connect back to our ancestors. But when my whanaunga asked me who I thought I was to use the name, I didn't argue the point. As it was, I had a back-up, which I was happy with, so in the end, I went with Te Aurere. The name comes from Aurere Beach, the stretch of beach on the other side of Awapoko River from my home.'

Seeing the waka afloat in Doubtless Bay was certainly a thrill for those who had travelled north to mark this launch. Photos from the day show Te Aurere, with her low, sleek lines, looking every inch the voyaging canoe. Nainoa Thompson reflects on the significance of the day for the Hawaiians: 'Just the fact that the canoe was finished was a huge accomplishment, but seeing her sitting on the beach, waiting for the tide to carry her into the sea was incredible. And for us to witness first hand the protocols that are associated with launching a waka was extremely powerful.'

Somewhat understandably, Hec's own memories of the day centre on the performance of the waka. He was far from content: 'To be honest it was all to hell. We couldn't even tack her. I think one of the reasons was because the hulls were still green – they were very heavy.' Additionally, one of Te Aurere's hulls was sitting lower in the water than the other: a result of the variation in size between the two kauri logs that Hec had been allocated. 'One of our logs was shorter than the other and it tapered quite quickly, so it was only about 2 foot 11 inches [87.5 centimetres] wide near the prow, while the other was closer to 3 foot 9 inches [1.125 metres]. Soon after the launch I had to strip the canoe right down so we could build up the front of the smaller hull by something like 10 inches [25 centimetres].' Hec also reduced the canoe's tendency to crab sideways under sail by adding a short keel to each hull.

With the alterations complete and Te Aurere's maiden coastal voyage to Waitangi successfully navigated, Hec sent out pānui to each of the waka crews who had participated in the 1990 sesquicentennial celebrations at Waitangi, inviting those interested to a series of training wānanga at Doubtless Bay.

As Marty Bercic recalls, Nainoa flew back for two or three wānanga early on to run sessions focusing predominantly on star identification: 'The aim of those early wānanga wasn't to try to teach us how to navigate, but rather how to use the stars to steer by. The crew needed to know what to do, for example, if the navigator told us he wanted to keep the star Antares at 90 degrees to the port hull for the next hour. So we learnt where each important star was, then we learnt where each of those stars sat in relation to lesser stars, so that we could still find our way should the main stars be hidden by cloud.'

On the occasions when Nainoa wasn't in the country, Stanley Conrad oversaw a series of wānanga that introduced basic sailing skills to prospective crew members. He also implemented the man-overboard drill that the Hawaiians were using. 'The drill was a critical part of the training,' recalls Stanley. 'Everyone needed to know what to do in an emergency. As soon as someone called "man overboard", every crew member had a specific job to do. Whoever was on the steering paddle turned the canoe into the wind, which stopped the waka. During daylight hours the crew member who saw the man fall overboard kept his eyes on him, or, if it happened at night, the man overboard pole needed to be thrown into the ocean as soon as possible. The pole was fitted with a long rope, a harness and two strobe lights, one of which was turned on before it was thrown into the ocean, the other after the person in the water had climbed into the harness. When the crew saw the two strobe lights flashing they would know their mate was ready to be pulled back to the waka.'

Participation in the various wānanga was all part and parcel of a selection process that eventually culminated in August 1992, when Hec announced the crew for the voyage to Rarotonga. Hec: 'In the lead-up to naming the crew I called a meeting of some of the guys I trusted to discuss who should make the final cut. It was important to get their feedback because I knew I couldn't keep an eye on everyone, and Nainoa had warned us to watch out for a few traits among the trainees. He told us to avoid guys who get too serious, or those who withdraw into themselves; and that you can't have guys on board who get moody because a waka is just too small.' Hec recalls that the meeting threw up one or two names, but in reality the crew largely picked itself. A number of those who had started attending the wānanga with enthusiasm had pulled out during the course of the year, and when Hec asked those still involved in the project whether they could commit fully to the voyage, it turned out that some couldn't get the three to four weeks off work that they would need for each leg.

Ultimately, Te Aurere's crew for the voyage to Rarotonga consisted of seven Māori – Stanley Conrad, Jack Thatcher, Paul Le Noel, Craig Subritzky, Sam Hauwaho, Te Aturangi Clamp and Pakake Winiata; master navigator Mau Piailug; Mau's nephew and interpreter Max Yarawamai; Piripi Evans, a kiwi who married into a branch of the Busby whānau; and the Hawaiian Clay Bertelmann. Hec also named five additional crew who would participate in the return voyage: Marty Bercic, Willie More and Hec's son Hector Junior, who would each sail to Rarotonga on the support boat *Nam Sang*, and Waingaroa (Magoo) Renata and Tai Mamaku, who would fly up. Hec himself didn't feature on either crew list: 'They didn't want me to have to suffer on board Te Aurere in the conditions they were expecting, and I didn't worry too much because I'd be on the support boat with the others, and at the end of the day we were all sailing together.'

Despite a lack of deep-water sailing experience among the crew, Hec felt comfortable with the final selection. In Clay Bertelmann he had a vastly experienced watch captain who would prove popular with the crew, while Mau Piailug was an unrivalled navigator and seaman.

While Hec respected Mau and his accomplishments, it wasn't until the Micronesian decided to stay with him at Aurere for several months preceding Te Aurere's maiden voyage that he really got to know him: 'I wasn't really living permanently at Aurere until early 1991, when the main house was moved to the site, so I'd only been there about ten months when Mau arrived – and with Hilda still working in Whāngārei during the week and only staying with me on the weekends, I was thankful for Mau's company. Actually, back then his English wasn't too good, but surprisingly we managed to communicate pretty well. He told me about his grandfather who was the one who taught him about navigation, and he would share interesting things from his people's waka culture, such as their habit of half-filling their waka with water if they were caught at sea by a hurricane. Mau explained that it helped to reduce the amount the vessel was thrown around, which I found very interesting. I picked up a lot of tips like that from Mau.'

Mau also offered priceless advice when it came time to lash Te Aurere, and later he was responsible for carving a series of compass points into the waka to aid with wayfinding. Hec: 'The markings allowed us to accurately line up guiding stars so the crew knew for sure that they were going in a certain direction. Say for instance we were heading north through the central Pacific, as we did during our 1995 voyage. Well, we knew

Mintaka rises on the equator, and if Mintaka was in line with the 90-degree mark on the starboard hull, then we knew we must be sailing north. And if we were meant to be heading to the north-east, then we'd line Mintaka up with our 45-degree mark.'

Mau's experience with waka didn't stop with full-sized canoes. He had made model sailing canoes for as long as he could remember, and he soon recognised that the flat waters of the Awapoko River behind his temporary home offered the perfect sailing environment. In the ample free time he had during his stay, Mau went about making a sleek model canoe, and fitted it with a custom-made sail. Sheltered from the stronger winds that buffeted the low rolling sandhills between the ocean and the river, his model canoe sped on light winds, traversing the width of the river to where eager hands would turn it around and set it free for the return voyage. The beautifully finished canoe's graceful performance mesmerised everyone who saw it sailing.

For Hec and his crew, watching the model canoe sail across the river was yet another reminder of the seemingly magical ability Mau possessed. Their people had lost even the most basic navigation skills and most of the techniques pertaining to both building and sailing voyaging canoes, but Mau was himself a repository of that very knowledge; a knowledge that had been passed down over many generations directly from his ancestors. This master navigator, skilled boatbuilder and experienced mariner understood both how to harness nature and when to bend to its will. He also knew only too well the dangers that the impending voyage could hold. In time, he would need to call upon all of his skills to see Te Aurere and her crew safely to Rarotonga. It would not be an easy voyage.

11

IN THE WAKE OF TŪMOANA

If Hec looked calm and collected to those around him in the days preceding Te Aurere's historic departure, it's probable that they weren't looking closely enough. 'The thought of all the responsibility on my shoulders kept running through my mind the whole time in the lead-up to the voyage. I knew that if anything happened to any of the crew I would have been in the gun. It was very, very tough right up until we left. In fact I was a little bit scared. If we lost anyone on that maiden voyage we would have been finished.'

Complicating matters was the September departure date. Hec would have preferred to sail in March, when the seas were calmer and the climate more suitable for voyaging north: 'That was when our ancestors sailed into the Pacific, leaving on the full moon tide at the same time the kūaka started its migration to Alaska, but of course the Festival of Pacific Arts was scheduled for mid-October, so we had no alternative other than to leave in late-September.' The choice as to whether to target the festival or wait for more settled weather in March had been tough for Hec. In the end he decided that the importance of having a voyaging waka represent Māori alongside waka from other Pacific nations outweighed the strong possibility that Te Aurere would encounter heavy seas on her voyage. It was a decision that would have repercussions.

As the scheduled departure date of 25 September approached, Hec kept an anxious eye on the weather, while Hilda began to supervise the loading of food and other supplies onto Te Aurere. Provisions were calculated based on the sail plan, which estimated Te Aurere would sail at an average of 4 knots per hour, or 96 miles per day. Enough supplies would be needed to feed the crew for eighteen days; in addition, emergency rations were planned to last an additional two weeks. Water supplies were carefully rationed as well: 2.5 litres of water were allowed per man per day. Hilda also organised provisions for Te Aurere's support boat, the *Nam Sang*. Once the darling of the racing world, the yacht had a colourful history. She was said to have been once owned by Paramount Film Studios, before becoming associated with a later owner's drug smuggling and mafia activities between California and South America.[1] Despite her checkered past, she seemed to be exactly what the expedition needed. She was fast and capable of sailing in heavy seas, and, importantly, she came with an experienced captain.

A windless morning greeted Hec when he awoke on the 25th. Much to everyone's frustration, conditions stayed that way for the remainder of the day. The 26th was no more productive, and in the late afternoon Mau, perhaps sensing the growing tension, called the crew together. Jack Thatcher recalls: 'Mau called a meeting a day or so before we left to pass on some waka lore from his homeland. One of the things he told us was to remember that the waka was our mother and she would always look after us, and that the navigator was our father, and if we ever needed anything, to ask him. It was just one of a number of sayings he shared with us leading into the voyage, and inevitably just at the right time, when things weren't going well or after you'd screwed up somehow, you'd remember some little gem he'd passed on – and it always seemed to help.'

When word finally came through on the 27th that the winds they were waiting on were expected the following day, Hec had Te Aurere brought around from Mangōnui Harbour and anchored her off the beach at Taipā.

As hoped, the next morning dawned fine, and the crew of Te Aurere were able to prepare for their departure under a warm sun. Once everything was stowed away securely and the crew members were back on shore, Hec recited his karakia, among many well-wishers. Stanley Conrad, who would be captaining the waka, recalls the emotion of the departure: 'Leaving our whānau and the old people was hard, especially knowing they would be worrying about us, but of course it was exciting at the same time. It was a big adventure that we had been building up to. And from a personal point of view there was a lot of pressure on me. I was the one who had sailed on Hōkūle'a, and none of the other Kiwis had that sort of experience – so I just wanted to get under way.'

With tears flowing freely, Te Aurere's crew, along with Hec, Marty Bercic, Willie More and Hector Junior, were ferried out to the waka to await the winds they had been promised. It would be a fruitless wait. Te Aurere, with its twin tauihu draped in wreaths and with streamers of native plants decorating the two taurapa at the rear, was eventually forced to motor out from the beach to rendezvous with the *Nam Sang* near the entrance to Mangōnui Harbour. Here, Hec and his three companions transferred to the yacht, joining Captain Brian Walden, owner Rich Brown, documentary maker Pita Turei and Pita's cameraman Mike Hardcastle aboard the 66-foot craft.

The winds remained elusive off the harbour entrance, and the decision was made to tow Te Aurere further offshore to see if the crew could locate their winds. It was an inauspicious departure, but nothing out of the ordinary for wind-borne vessels. Within minutes of the decision, however, the captain of the *Nam Sang* was forced to radio Te Aurere to explain that their motor was playing up. Unbelievably, the gearbox had been put in back to front during the yacht's pre-voyage tune-up, and they would have to make for port to have it repaired. Needless to say it was a deflated crew that made its way to Whangaroa.

Finally, early on the morning of 29 September, the two vessels were able to start their voyage with sails set in a moderate breeze, the *Nam Sang* off Te Aurere's port hull. Behind them lay Aotearoa and loved ones. Ahead lay the uncertainty of adventure on the open Pacific. It would be a voyage that would surely test Te Aurere and her novice crew to the limit.

The sail plan for the voyage was simple enough: sail 1000 miles due east, turn north towards the equator, and then run before strong southerlies that would speed them to Rarotonga. All things going well, the course would see Te Aurere avoid the worst of the frequent winter storms that have haunted sailors for centuries and get them to Rarotonga in time for the festival's official welcome.

Life on board Te Aurere soon settled into a predictable routine for the crew as they edged their way out into the vast Pacific Ocean. For much of the first week, time on deck during each six-hour watch was spent under fair skies. It was a relaxed introduction, and one that was appreciated by the senior crew members who knew an easing-in period was exactly what the novice crew needed. The fine weather had one downside, however. In the quieter moments, some members of the crew became fixated on the constant flow of noises emanating from the vessel. Jack: 'The creaks and moans were a little disturbing to be honest. They hadn't been nearly so noticeable on our day trips before the voyage, but during that first week I was always conscious of the noises, especially at night. It wasn't until Mau and Clay explained that it was just the various parts of the waka working together to dissipate the stress that the canoe was under that I started to relax.'

It was a valuable period of calm, but one that didn't last. A week out from port, the weather changed abruptly: strengthening winds ushered in a series of nasty squalls that quickly developed into a raging storm. Jack: 'When the first storm hit we were all up on deck watching every wave come in, and there were some huge waves that crashed right over us. It was the first time most of us had experienced storm conditions, and we were mesmerised.' The roar of the storm seemed to intensify for the crew as night fell, and the inability to see incoming waves didn't help with growing unease among many of the rookie sailors. Exposed to truly rough weather for the first time, those on watch duty quickly learnt there was nowhere to hide when roiling rivers of cold water washed across the kauri decking. 'To be honest, we didn't know what to expect when that first storm hit us,' continues Jack, 'and we weren't really sure how the waka was going to handle it. It quickly became quite a terrifying experience. The reality for us was that we had only once sailed outside of Doubtless Bay in our nine months of training, and that was to go diving for seafood around the corner at Karikari Peninsula.'

Things weren't any more comfortable for Hec and the others on the *Nam Sang*: conditions on the yacht deteriorated as soon as the first squalls arrived. Hec: 'It was a beautiful boat, but it turned out that it hadn't been looked after. It was leaking like hell – through the roof and all over the bloody place – and we had the pump going all the time. In fact, when it came time to sleep below decks we had to wrap ourselves in whatever we could to try to stay dry. I had my oilskin, but a couple of the others had to resort to using spare sails.' To top things off, the crew had to contend with a minor diesel spill that left below decks reeking for much of the voyage.

The storm barely lasted a day, but it was a real enough introduction to what the Pacific Ocean could throw at the waka. Pakake Winiata later described the conditions on board Te Aurere as similar to walking around with a trickling hose down your front and your back: 'It was twenty-four-hour a day wet.'[2]

Nevertheless, the worst of the weather was behind them, and life on board Te Aurere soon returned to normal. Each change of shift was routinely announced with a half-hour warning call and then a five-minute reminder. Then, after they had assembled on deck, the first task of the incoming watch inevitably involved pumping out any water that had seeped into the hulls since the previous changeover. Once that was completed, the crew were free to make themselves as comfortable as possible while they waited for the first of their two or three half-hour stints on the steering paddle.

Cooking duties, shared by Clay and Jack and performed on the open deck, recommenced, having become next to impossible during the high winds, as did the fishing. Jack: 'We caught a lot of fish on trawling lures on the way up – tuna, albacore, wahoo and mahimahi. I remember at one point the crew of the *Nam Sang* asking us for half a tuna we had just pulled in, and they came alongside and threw over a rope to tie the fish onto. Unfortunately while Piripi was head-down, securing the fish to the line, the two craft started to drift apart, and just as he threw the fish in for them to pull across, the *Nam Sang* ran out of rope, and down went the fish and about 100 metres of line! That was a bit of a laughing point for a few nights after: "Hey Piripi, throw us a line, but don't forget to hold on to the other end bro!"'

The respite from the rough weather was short-lived; within two days, Te Aurere found herself caught in the centre of three converging storm fronts. 'We were happily sailing along in fair winds, with most of us unaware of what was happening around us: that was until Mau pointed out what was coming our way,' recalls Jack. 'Up to the north-east there were dense black clouds, and to the south there was another system, and behind us was yet another one. Well, our first thought was that Mau was awesome for being able to read that, and it wasn't until we actually started watching the weather close in around us that we thought, Oh shit! Up until then we hadn't yet put two and two together to come up with a bloody big storm.'

Mau instinctively grasped that the most sensible course of action was to try and outflank one of the converging storm fronts, and he asked Stanley Conrad to change the canoe's heading to the north-west. With luck, this course might allow them to slip through a small gap between two of the fronts and escape the worst of the weather. Within minutes of changing direction, however, Te Aurere received an urgent call from the *Nam Sang*. Hec was demanding to know who had given the authority for them to change course. Jack: 'I can't remember his exact words, but I think Mau's reply was something like, "Did you say I don't know where I go?" and then he got a bit brassed off and basically told us to stop, pull all our gear down and to wait out the storm. Of course we were all thinking, Mau must know what he's doing, let's just get the hell out of here. But instead we sat there waiting for the storm to arrive. By four o'clock the swell had started to grow to 3–4 metres, and the wind was reaching 25–30 knots, and we're thinking, Oh, it's not so bad if it stays like this. It'll be sweet. But it continued to get worse until getting on towards dark the wind was about 45–50 knots and the swell was huge. By that stage we were gripping the rails like we had claws.'

Adding to the drama was the fact that the *Nam Sang* couldn't heave-to in the same manner as Te Aurere, and the two vessels soon drifted apart, remaining both out of view and out of radio contact for the best part of three days. The stress of the situation

Hec, Hilda and Nainoa's father, Myron 'Pinky' Thompson. Pinky was a long-time social worker in Hawai'i before becoming a respected cultural leader among the Native Hawaiians. His example of working for his people undoubtedly helped mould Nainoa into the leader he would become.
Photo supplied by Busby family

Hec beside a carving in Alaska, 1990. The trip to Alaska would afford Hec the opportunity to meet with elders who had a deep connection to their ancestral land. Nainoa would later comment that the combined group of elders, 'spoke a very deep native language', and he was impressed by how easily Hec joined in their discussions.
Photo supplied by Busby family

Te Aurere in her white undercoat and with her single mast soon after launching in January 1992. She would prove hard to manoeuvre on the day, due in part to the unequal size of her hulls, and she soon showed a tendency to crab under sail, a flaw Hec partially remedied by adding a short keel to the underside of each hull.
Photo supplied by Busby family

The crew of Te Aurere show off their wet weather gear on the waka beside the prominently displayed banner from sponsor Lifespan Smokefree.
Photo supplied by Busby family

A weary Hec taking his turn on the wheel of the *Nam Sang*. Hammered by a week-long storm and separated from Te Aurere for days on end, the maiden voyage to Rarotonga in 1992 seriously affected Hec's health to the point that he was unable to join the crew for the return voyage.
Photo supplied by Busby family

Te Aurere arriving in Rarotonga to an enthusiastic welcome, October 1992. Grave fears had been held for the safety of the crew as radio calls from Avarua went unanswered for over a week. A signal from Te Aurere's escort boat, the *Nam Sang*, was finally picked up in Rarotonga a few days before the official welcoming ceremony was scheduled.
Photo supplied by Busby family

A storm-ravaged Te Aurere arrives home to a wonderful reception after her voyage to Rarotonga. What many of those waiting on the beach didn't realise at the time was that Te Aurere had been the victim of a freak wave, and she was missing 6 feet of her mast.
Photo supplied by Busby family

Crew and supporters of Te Aurere in Tahiti 1995. Front row in white (l–r): Hilda Busby, Te Ao Pehi Kara and Waiariki Kara. Hec is standing, fifth from the left. *Photo supplied by Stanley Conrad*

Te Aurere, escorted by a local outrigger racing canoe, enters Te Avemo'a pass off shore from Taputapuatea Marae, Ra'iatea, 1995.
Photo copyright Ben Finney

Te Ao Pehi Kara leads Hec and crew ashore at Ra'iatea, 1995. Invited by Hec to perform the tapu-lifting karakia during the ceremony at Taputapuatea Marae, Te Ao Pehi was able to call upon a deep basket of traditional knowledge. The historic tapu-lifting ceremony was witnessed by thousands of locals.
Photo copyright Ben Finney

Hec, Stanley Conrad and Jack Thatcher lead Te Aurere's crew ashore at Nuku Hiva in 1995. Stanley carries a mauri stone from Aotearoa, a symbol of both friendship and a shared cultural history.
Photo copyright Monte Costa

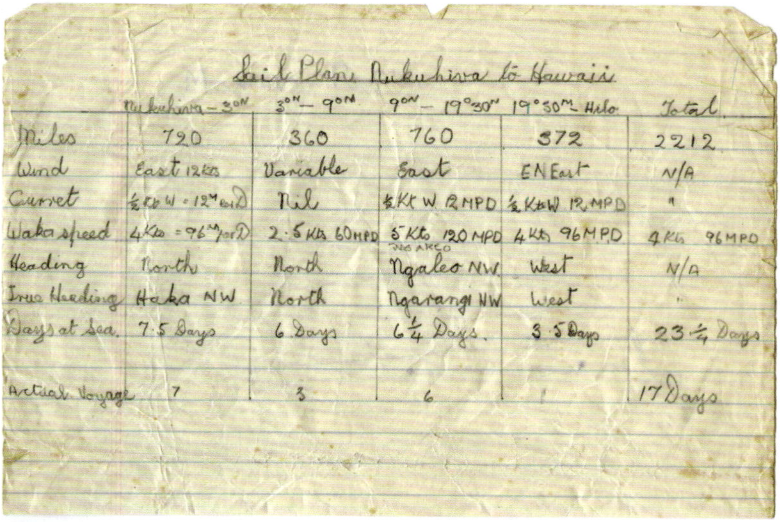

Sail Plan Nukuhiva to Hawaii

	Nukuhiva – 3°N	3°N – 9°N	9°N – 19°30'N	19°30'N – Hilo	Total
Miles	720	360	760	372	2212
Wind	East 12Kts	Variable	East	ENEast	N/A
Current	½ Kt W = 12M a D	Nil	½ Kt W 12 MPD	½ Kt W 12 MPD	"
Waka speed	4Kts = 96M per D	2.5 Kts 60 MPD	5 Kts 120 MPD	4 Kts 96 MPD	4 Kts 96 MPD
Heading	North	North	Ngaleo NW	West	N/A
True Heading	Haka NW	North	Ngarangi NW	West	"
Days at Sea.	7.5 Days	6 Days	6¼ Days.	3.5 Days	23¼ Days
Actual Voyage	7	3	6	1	17 Days

The sail plan for the voyage from Nuku Hiva to Hawa'i, 1995. Divided into four legs, the sail plan takes into account such variables as expected waka speed and currents to estimate how many days it will take to sail to Hawai'i. That estimation, in turn, helps determine how much food and water will be carried on the waka.
Supplied by Hec Busby

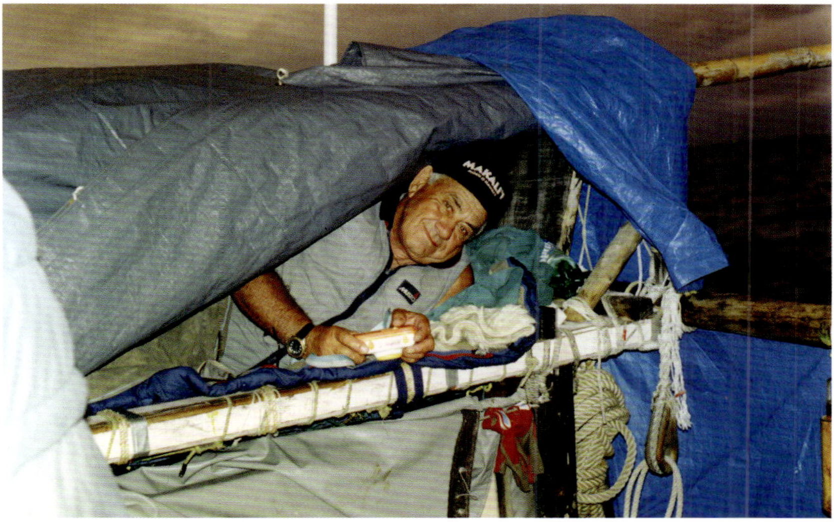

Hec resting in his favoured spot atop Te Aurere's bunks during the 1995 voyage. The makeshift set-up allowed the crew instant access to him should they need to consult with him while he was off duty and ensured he was in close proximity to the steersman and navigator should he sense the waka wandering off course.
Photo copyright Robert Gable

Hec and sailor, author and adventurer David Lewis aboard Te Aurere. Lewis's book *We, the Navigators* was a significant factor in the renaissance of Polynesian navigation. He sailed on Te Aurere on the 1995 leg from Rarotonga to Aotearoa. After his death, in February 2003, his ashes were scattered from Te Aurere on Auckland's Waitemata Harbour.
Photo supplied by Busby family

Te Aurere arriving at Anakena Beach, Rapa-nui, during the Waka Tapu voyage. Having reached Hawai'i in 1995, Hec was determined that Te Aurere should close the Polynesian Triangle before she was retired. He would witness her make land at the isolated island in 2013.
Photo supplied by Busby family

Hec's second voyaging canoe, Ngāhiraka Mai Tawhiti, being manhandled through the shallows of Awapoko River at the end of the arduous Waka Tapu voyage, 2013.
Photo by author

Legends of the sea: Hec with Nainoa Thompson, Waitangi, November 2014.
Photo by author

soon took a toll on Hec's health, which deteriorated to such an extent that there were serious concerns among those on the support boat. A photograph of Hec taken at the helm of the *Nam Sang* at this stage of the voyage clearly shows his fatigue. His drawn face is partially hidden under a salt-and-pepper beard, and deep lines are carved across his forehead. As Hector Junior confirms, his father lost a considerable amount of weight on the trip: 'mainly after the two boats separated during the storm. He was really worrying about the guys on the waka, and even though he isn't a person who shows his emotions, I knew what was happening in his head. He stressed out a lot during that trip.'

While Hec was dealing with the pressure as best he could on the *Nam Sang*, the crew aboard Te Aurere were forced to sit out the storm in cold and uncomfortable conditions. It was an unnerving experience for most of the crew, but Mau and Clay had been through as much before, and it was clear that they trusted the waka to survive the beating it was receiving. Their assured demeanour meant that those on board remained composed in the face of growing seas. Stanley: 'We were being absolutely hammered by the storm, and everyone who could took shelter in a bunk. Those who missed out huddled on deck trying to keep out of the wind as best they could because it was freezing. To say it was uncomfortable is an understatement.'

Adding to the crew's woes was a sharp decline in the number of fish being caught; this was especially rough when they realised that the only substitute for fresh fish that they had was a large supply of tinned lamb's tongue. Jack: 'Apparently Hilda had asked Stanley in the run-up to the voyage what meat he thought the crew would enjoy on the trip, and being a good farm boy Stanley had suggested lamb's tongue. Well, Hilda took him at his word and purchased cans and cans of the stuff, so we were stuck with eating lamb's tongue once the fishing dropped away. It's a bit of an acquired taste, but what made it worse, especially for us cooks, was seeing the skin peel away when we pulled the tongues out of the cans!'

When the two craft finally found each other, Hec radioed Stanley and informed him that he had decided to take Te Aurere under tow and head to the south-east. 'After seven days we were only 50 miles further on from where we entered the storm, so I decided to tow Te Aurere to try to find the westerlies we needed.' It had not been a simple decision to make. Reports from New Zealand were suggesting that the way to escape the grip of the storm was to head to the south-east, which would return Te Aurere to the original course line, but Hec was also well aware that in Mau he had an acknowledged master navigator who had spent a life on the water, and Mau wanted to sail to the north-west.

On reflection, it seems the main cause of the initial conflict between the two craft had been a simple misunderstanding about the purpose of the predetermined course line. From day one, Hec had wanted to stick to the original easterly course so he could use the forecast southerlies far to the east of Aotearoa to get the two vessels up to Rarotonga. He also knew that if they continued heading on the north-westerly course that Mau favoured, the two craft would have difficulty reaching Rarotonga in the required time frame, given the wind patterns expected further north. In Jack's estimation, sailing to the north-west was straying too far from the course line for Hec. 'Being so inexperienced at the time, I don't think any of us Kiwis really understood that departures from the course line are necessary in certain instances: that you don't have to hold to your exact course line 100 per cent of the time. You can actually make a deviation because of threatening weather, but the idea is that you keep a mental track of your progress and then as long as you know where you are at any time, you can eventually make your way back to your course line.'

Adding to the tension was a growing unrest among the crew of Te Aurere, who were far from happy when they were instructed to tie up to the *Nam Sang*. They became even more upset when it became clear to them that they were being shepherded further from their final destination and into increasingly rough weather. Jack: 'In the end we were getting quite despondent ... we spoke to the *Nam Sang* during one of the scheduled evening calls a couple of days after they started to tow us. We told them that Mau still wanted to go to the north-west, and that we believed we should listen to what he was saying. We reiterated that we had always thought that Mau was going to be the guide for the waka, and that wasn't happening. Mau continued the conversation with Hec, and I remember he said something like: "No. No. I am looking at the weather. Everything is telling me storms to the south. We don't want to go there." In the end Hec conceded and agreed to sail to the north-west. We hove to and waited for morning before we set off. Well, within a day the weather had cleared, and we got favourable winds. It seemed quite miraculous to us at the time. We were able to drop the tow and went back to sailing – and our spirits rose dramatically. All of a sudden we were getting good winds and the sun was out, so we went from this crew low on morale after having the stuffing knocked out of us for a number of days to a happy bunch enjoying life again. Whether the winds would have turned up if we had carried on to the south no one knows, but we felt we had taken a positive step by listening to our navigator.'

Along with the improved weather came an improvement in the crew's appetite, as Jack recalls: 'Stanley's mum made us some apple pies for the trip, and we had a wicked feed during the first few days of the voyage. They were so nice that I decided we should save some for later in the journey in case we needed pepping up, so I put six of them away. Well, one night a couple of weeks into the trip I was hunting through our supplies to give my watch a midnight feast when I found the pies stashed away. They were delicious, and we ended up eating four of them. When the other fellas came up for their shift the next morning I said to them, "I found those apple pies and left a couple for you." Well, they knew I had put away six and they were a little bit dirty on us – until they cut into the pies and saw that they were full of green mould!'

The calmer weather allowed the crew to take stock of the canoe's condition. Of major concern were the steering paddles, which were struggling to stand up to the rigours of open-ocean voyaging, and making it difficult for the crew to keep Te Aurere on course. Additionally, the weight of the storm-tossed waves had ripped much of the canvas covering the bunks, and some of the crew were left with unobstructed views of the ocean as they drifted off to sleep in their hammocks. Better weather also gave crew members an opportunity to attend to issues of personal hygiene, as Jack explains: 'We were constantly wet and had nowhere to go to get out of the storm other than to lie in our bunks, and that made changing out of wet, clingy clothes next to impossible, so we ended up living in the same gear for days on end. And on top of that we really weren't able to wash during the storm, so you can imagine we were paru as when we were finally able to take off our wet-weather gear.'

The drama of the storm had been played out against a running clock, and by the time Te Aurere had found the sea breezes she needed it was looking likely that she would miss the official welcome on 21 October. That likelihood was confirmed a few days later when Hec finally managed to make radio contact with Rarotonga. 'When we finally got a call through to Rarotonga Hilda happened to be there at the radio operator's side. It was wonderful to hear her voice, half-laughing and half-crying, and to be able to let all of our loved ones know we were safe. They had been hailing us for close to a week without receiving a reply, so she was relieved to finally hear from me. That was when we learnt that the official welcoming ceremony for the canoes was going to proceed in three days' time, which forced me to make another tough decision: we needed to tow Te Aurere again to try to make the ceremony. Basically the extra horsepower from the tow was going to add a further 2 knots to our speed, or an additional 48 miles each day, and that gave us an outside chance of getting to Rarotonga in time. On top of that, the steering paddles were a real problem and making it next to impossible to stay on course.' Jack: 'So we were under the tow again, which tore the adventure out of the whole thing, but at least Mau was back navigating and instructing the *Nam Sang* which direction to tow us.'

It was the experienced pairing of Mau and Clay who first sighted the peaks of Rarotonga at dawn on 22 October, the morning after the official welcoming ceremony, as Pakake Winiata recounts: 'The rest of us were looking everywhere but straight ahead, and it was another four hours before we spotted it, like a cloud on the horizon, dead ahead.' As they closed in on the island the crew became fixated on the clouds congregating above its dominating peak, Maungatea. Clouds had always been one of the primary signs that navigators sought out when they sailed between islands; they magnify an island's height by reflecting the hues of lush vegetation from below, and clumps of cloud frequently appear to be magnetised above an island while other clouds further out continue to be pushed before the winds. This phenomenen is often visible in photos of Rarotonga and other high islands throughout the Pacific.

As the two craft came within a few miles of Rarotonga, Hec transferred to Te Aurere so he could complete the karakia he had begun back at Taipā, the final verse of which released the kaitiaki who had looked after the waka and crew during the voyage. Then, escorted by the magnificent 27.6-metre Rarotongan war canoe Uritaua, Te Aurere made her way around to Ngātangi'ia. 'It was a beautiful day,' recalls Hec, 'and there were thousands of people along the waterfront. It looked like the whole of the island had come out to greet us.'

As the crew walked ashore to the beat of island drums, they could afford to stand proud. They had lasted the voyage on the first waka to journey from New Zealand to Rarotonga in nearly seven centuries. Two decades after the fact, Stanley Conrad puts his thoughts about the day into words: 'We were excited to get there and to fulfil the dreams that our people had held since Hōkūle'a arrived in Aotearoa. We had sailed to Rarotonga on our own waka, and the crew went through a lot to get there. I felt we had achieved something – pulled something off – and the fact that we had our own welcoming ceremony made it all the more special.'

Hec's most vivid memories of the day come from the arrival on the beach: 'Oh my gosh. I tell you it was a very, very emotional welcome, especially when I was embraced by the Māori Queen. I don't remember her saying much when we embraced, but she cried and cried and wouldn't let me go. And of course the kapa haka group Waka Huia and the crew of our waka taua Te Ika a Māui were on the island as part of the offical Te Waka Toi delegation, and they performed a haka for us right there on the beach.'

Whether everyone in attendance that afternoon was aware of the historical significance of Te Aurere's arrival is unknown, but no one could have underestimated the importance of their achievement after listening to the Cook Islands Prime Minister Geoffrey Henry welcome Hec and the crew. As Hec recalls, Henry's speech started with a salutation welcoming them home: 'The gist of his speech went something like: "Welcome home. Over 700 years ago your ancestors left here to voyage to Aotearoa, and today you have finally arrived back. So drink deep from the niu [coconut]. It is the drink of your ancestors." Oh – that really hit me. I just had to let the tears run. It was a hell of a welcome.'

The ceremony was concluded in fading light when Hec, resplendent in a feather cloak and woven headband, placed a stone mauri from Doubtless Bay alongside those laid the previous day by the crews of the other voyaging canoes. The homecoming was complete.

For much of the following week the crew caught up with family and friends and fulfilled speaking engagements at the festival and local schools, and a few of them enjoyed the unique experience of paddling a waka taua in the waters of Rarotonga. There was also the serious matter of a debrief to attend to. 'In the end the big issue for a lot of us on Te Aurere wasn't that we were towed so much as the direction we were towed, which overruled where our navigator wanted to go,' recalls Jack. 'At the time we were adamantly against being towed to the south-east, and we explained why during the debrief, but the discussion always came back to Hec's insistence that we needed to stay as close to the course line as possible.'

From Hec's perspective, the need to follow the advice coming from the professionals on land was paramount: 'We were stuck in the storm for seven days, hardly moving, and the Met office back in New Zealand was telling us to sail south-east to get out of the storm. It was as simple as that.'

The crew also discussed the fact that neither Mau nor Clay would be returning to New Zealand on Te Aurere. For some that was too much to come to terms with, as Marty Bercic recalls: 'One or two said that they wouldn't go back if Mau wasn't sailing, so we dealt with that by simply telling them they didn't have to, that we'd fly them home. The majority of us believed that the first leg had shown us where we needed to improve, and besides, at the end of the day we still had to get Te Aurere back home for the old fella.'

The second week in Rarotonga started with a concerted effort by the crew to rebuild the waka's sleeping quarters and to check the rest of the canoe for seaworthiness – and it finished with a night out on the town organised by Marty. 'We had been behaving ourselves at the festival because we were representing New Zealand,' Marty recalls, 'but by the end of our second week on the island just about everyone had gone home, so I decided the time was right for a blow-out to gee everyone up. To be honest some of us were still a bit shell-shocked from the sail over, and I figured we needed some gelling time together. I had a full wallet from a redundancy payout, so we headed to a local cocktail bar by the airport and emptied the shelves.'

Two days later, on the morning of 7 November, Te Aurere quietly raised her sail and set a course for home. Magoo Renata, Marty Bercic, Willy More, Tai Mamaku and Hector Junior had joined the crew, replacing Mau, Max Yarawamai, Clay Bertelmann, Paul Le Noel, Sam Hauwaho and Pakake Winiata. The vessel would once again be captained by Stanley Conrad, who would run one watch in partnership with Piripi Evans, while Jack Thatcher was appointed the second watch captain.

Once again there was no room for Hec. He had suffered during the voyage to Rarotonga – in part through the stress of worrying about Te Aurere and her crew, and in part, perhaps, through the conflict with Mau – and he hadn't yet fully recovered. Marty admits the crew were disappointed that Hec couldn't accompany them, but they knew that if they encountered another storm it might have had serious consequences for him. 'He was a little heartbroken that he couldn't come back with us, but he accepted the reality that he was a sixty-year-old and that he really needed time to recover.' Hec was very matter-of-fact about missing out on the voyage home. He considered himself 'a canoe builder at that point in time, and not really part of the voyaging crew'; he hadn't expected to be on board. Although the idea of voyaging in the Pacific was tempting, Hec knew deep down he needed to rest, and that the job of sailing Te Aurere home was best left to the others.

As Rarotonga sank into the ocean behind them the crew gave silent thanks for the fair weather they had been blessed with, and settled into their routines. The pleasant conditions held for the first two weeks of the voyage, allowing the crew to spend much of their free time on deck enjoying themselves in tropical warmth rather than hunkering down out of the wind and rain. As Jack recalls, cards became a regular pastime in the evenings. Chocolates and lollies, introduced to help ward off the constant taste of salt in the crew's mouths, became a treasured currency: 'When we were off duty it was "Deal up, boys". One of these lollies is worth two of those ones. One of these is worth two of these and two of those, and a chocolate bar is five of those and five of them. So when someone bet you five hard-boiled lollies and a chocolate bar, there was real pressure to decide whether he had good cards or not.'

When freshening winds arrived near the tail end of the second week no one thought much of them: the winds were pushing Te Aurere ever closer to home, and didn't seem overly threatening.

'We started off doing about 90 miles a day,' remembers Stanley, 'but by two weeks out we were flying, doing 140 miles a day. In fact things were going well until perhaps two days' sail from North Cape, when the first clue that the weather might be about to change for the worse came along. A pod of forty to fifty dolphins came racing past us from the direction we were headed. We were already in a decent swell, and they were flying 20–30 feet across the troughs. Well, we were completely mesmerised by them, but we really should have been asking ourselves why they were running and not stopping to play with us.'

Within half an hour another storm had fallen upon them, forcing Stanley to order all sails to be dropped. Marty: 'At its worst the waves were breaking from all directions and there was no escaping the noise, except when every once in a while it went silent … and then you'd hear Jack shouting, "Incoming!" Then there would be a big boom as the wave broke over the canoe. To be honest I still don't know what was worse: the silence or Jack screaming! We were only on the edge of the worst of it, but even so the winds were constantly above 60 knots and gusting up to 100 at times.' Jack: 'For long periods we had everyone up on deck with safety lines attached and life jackets on. Waves were breaking over the canoe, and whenever a big one broke over us we would yell out everyone's name to make sure we were all accounted for.'

If that wasn't enough excitement for the battered crew, late the following day an urgent shout rang out on the craft: 'Holy hell, there's a container ship coming at us!' With the storm still raging around them, one of the crew had picked out a distant 'thuga, thuga, thuga,' piercing the gloom. Stanley: 'Well, the radio was playing up a bit, so we put all our pots and pans up by our radar reflector, and then someone pulled out our flare guns and held them like a couple of six shooters, joking that at least we'd go down fighting.' It was with relief that they watched the ship pass well clear of their position; given the conditions there was little doubt that all hands would probably have been lost had they collided.

When the wind finally started to drop in intensity on the third morning, the crew, anxious to get under way, set their storm sail and turned their waka towards home. The two-day delay had been unfortunate, but was soon forgotten: within a couple of hours, a rogue wave was causing more havoc. Jack Thatcher was in the thick of it: 'Magoo was on the steering paddle when a swell picked us up and suddenly we were in trouble again. I fell and knocked him off his feet, and before we knew it there were three or four of us on top of each other down against the rails. And when we looked up, the mast and sail were gone!'

The tangled mess was a depressing sight, and for the next hour the crew worked to recover the mast and sail from the ocean. The *Nam Sang*, once again taking on water, had already run for port, so the only realistic option they had if they wanted to sail Te Aurere home was to repair the mast as best they could and crawl along under a jury rig. Still at least a day and a half from home, and with the seas still running high, it was a disconsolate crew that came to the realisation they would have to call for assistance. Jack: 'They were less than ideal sailing conditions for a crippled waka, and we realised pretty early on that we would be struggling to make New Zealand, so Stanley made the call.'

Fortunately a well-appointed tuna boat was in Te Aurere's vicinity at the time of the incident, and was able to locate her within a matter of hours. 'Despite the disappointment, we were still hoping the boat would take a while to arrive so we could at least set up the jury rig and see if we could make some headway,' remembers Jack, 'but next thing you know we were under tow again, chugging along at 11–12 knots, heading for Mangōnui Harbour.

After the trials of the last two days, it was an emotional homecoming for the crew when they reached Aurere on the morning of 26 November. Mataatua-Puhi met them out in the bay and escorted them to shore, while hundreds of well-wishers and family stood among the sand dunes to greet them. Stanley: 'It was amazing coming home to our own people and stepping back on our own whenua at Aurere. We had sailed back without Mau, Clay or Max, and it was just a crew of Māori. What was really important to us was that the voyage had reassured our old people by supporting the stories that were connected to our whakapapa and genealogy. It upheld the voyaging traditions of our ancestors, our tūpuna.'

Their arrival home was in truth the culmination of an incredible achievement – especially on Hec's part. In a little under two years, and with no prior experience constructing double-hulled voyaging canoes, Hec had built Te Aurere, tested and refined her, seen to the selection and training of her crew, and organised her voyage to Rarotonga and back. In short, he had indeed succeeded in building a canoe capable of following in the wake of his ancestor Tūmoana. Inevitably mistakes had been made during the voyage, but what mattered to Hec was that the waka had proven itself capable in testing conditions, and the crew had returned safe and well.

Te Aurere's arrival home did not signal the end of her voyaging days; Hec's thoughts had already turned to optimising her sailing performance. There was undoubtedly room for improvement, and improvements would be made. Hec: 'I started to work on her a couple of weeks after she got back, adding a second mast, which was easy enough, but she was also still drifting sideways while under sail, and sorting that out took some time. That wasn't minimised until we added lee boards.'

If Hec had hoped for an extended period to work on his waka and recuperate out of the public's eye after the voyage, it wasn't to be. On 8 February 1993, just two and a half months after Te Aurere's return, Television New Zealand announced to the nation that the canoe had been towed part of the way to Rarotonga. The story implied that Te Aurere's crew had cheated, had tried to keep the towing secret, and had been found out. In fact, this was far from true. Radio contact between the *Nam Sang* and maritime radio services in both Rarotonga and New Zealand had openly discussed the occasions when Te Aurere had been under tow. Hec: 'I was disgusted when I heard the reports, because there was never any hiding of the towing. All of our broadcasts over the radio stated, "under tow as we are making no head way", or, "under tow because we are late", so we were quite open about the towing. What's more, we also mentioned it during speeches in Rarotonga.'

The integrity of the television report was challenged on the front page of the *New Zealand Herald* on 9 February in an article in which Hec reiterated that, yes, Te Aurere had been towed, but that it had never been kept a secret; and that the towing had been acknowledged 'on stepping ashore at Rarotonga'. He went on to explain to the *Herald* reporter that Te Aurere had been tied to the *Nam Sang* during the storm to stop the two craft from separating, and that 'the *Nam Sang* took the waka under tow towards the end of the journey when one of its steering paddles broke'. The article quoted part owner of the *Nam Sang*, Rich Brown, who had sailed on the vessel throughout the voyage, confirming that Te Aurere had sailed 'most of the way on their own'. In another article, published on 12 February, the *Nam Sang*'s captain, Brian Walden, joined in, pointing out that the crew members of Te Aurere were the first Māori to venture to sea in a waka in hundreds of years, and deserved credit, not criticism: 'We have to remember that these people don't have the experience of their ancestors. If I was descended from Captain Cook I couldn't automatically sail around The Cape.'

Despite the anger it caused at the time, the television report ultimately made Hec and his core crew members a stronger, more resolute unit. Determined to build on their experience, Hec organised for his most promising crew members to spend time with Nainoa Thompson learning to navigate. What Hec wanted now was a home-grown navigator.

Notes

[1] *New Zealand Herald*, 11 September 1993, p. 9.

[2] McDonald, M. 'A Voyage of Rediscovery', *Mana* magazine, April/May 1993, p.39.

12

REOPENING ANCIENT SEA PATHS

In July 1993, Stanley Conrad, Jack Thatcher, Marty Bercic and Piripi Evans accompanied Hec on the first of several trips to Hawai'i. Hec had arranged the visits as part of a concerted effort to prepare his crew for Te Aurere's next Pacific expedition, the Polynesian Voyaging Society's collective voyage, Nā 'Ohana Holo Moana (the Voyaging Families of the Vast Ocean), which was scheduled for 1995 and timed to coincide with the launching of Hawai'iloa, the Society's new waka. For the New Zealanders, the trip would be the beginning of an exhaustive two and a half years spent studying traditional navigation with Nainoa. 'My most intense contribution towards Hector's programme has been the training of the navigators,' says Nainoa. 'On their first trip up to Hawai'i we introduced them to the simple stuff, starting with the stars, which they obviously had to learn in more depth than any of the other crew members. Having said that it's the simple stuff, it still takes commitment to learn. You have to spend time studying the stars to understand how the shape of the sky moves.' Among the other skills that new navigators needed to master was the ability to interpret the numerous clues to be found in the ocean, such as wave patterns and ocean currents. 'Of all the things I have passed on they're the biggest challenge to teach,' Nainoa explains, 'because signs at sea are very complicated things to read, as we all see the world differently. I can look at the ocean and I'll read it a certain way, but the guy standing right next to me can be looking at the same thing and read it totally differently.'

Nainoa also introduced the New Zealanders to the finer points of producing sail plans for long-distance voyages, including the need to take into account expected weather conditions, the anticipated strength of currents along the way and the predicted speed of the waka. 'It was,' according to Nainoa, 'a serious commitment for all involved.'

The opportunity to learn directly from Nainoa was a generous gift, as were the places allotted to Hec's men aboard Hawai'iloa and Hōkūle'a during several training voyages. It wasn't always a standard learning environment, however. During one particular voyage, Nainoa, who was the principal navigation instructor on board, dived off the canoe as they sailed past South Point, the southernmost point of Hawai'i, and left them to it. As Jack recalls: 'We were starting out on a two-week voyage and Nainoa jumped off and left me! Well, at least that's how I felt. Although there were a few of us trainee navigators on board at the time, all I could think was: Where's the beggar going? What's he doing? I mean we were supposed to be learning from this guy, and he jumps off the waka and leaves us to sail by ourselves.' Nainoa later explained that he didn't want to be a crutch for the rookies to lean on: 'He wanted us to learn for ourselves, rather than have him there to fall back on,' says Jack. 'He thought that we wouldn't be able to learn as much if he was out there with us, and he was probably right.'

If it seemed to family and friends that Hec and his senior crew members were spending a lot of time in exotic locations, they were right. During one particular twelve-month period Hec travelled to Hawai'i five times, including spending a week helping Nainoa dig the foundations for his bach on the Big Island at Kona, not far from the Captain Cook memorial. During this period Hec began to study navigation seriously for the first time: 'I decided to learn to navigate the old way soon after Jack, Piripi and the boys started training with the Hawaiians. Up to that point I had only seen myself as a canoe builder, or perhaps a crew member. I remember it was actually quite intimidating when I started with Nainoa, because I'd never bothered about stars before that. I didn't even know where the Southern Cross was back then.' Fortunately for Hec he lived in the perfect location to study the stars; his home at Aurere enjoyed skies unaffected by big city lights and he had almost unobstructed views across Doubtless Bay to the eastern horizon. Before long, what had once been an unfocused haze in the night sky became intricate patterns that he often learnt by the Hawaiian, Māori and scientific names.

Hec also began to read up on Kupe, acknowledged by most tribes as the navigator who discovered Aotearoa. 'His situation was a little bit different to ours, of course,' explains Hec, 'because he didn't know how far away Aotearoa was when he went looking for it. He would have known that there was land down here after studying migrating land-based birds, though, and he knew what direction to sail because when migrating birds leave one island for another they fly directly to their destination. Once he understood that, all he had to do was to align the direction the birds were flying with the heavens, and he had his course. What Kupe discovered during his voyage was that both the sun and Venus set in the general direction that the birds were flying during November and December – so, as we are told in our traditions, the sun and Venus became his principal guiding bodies. I've checked it all out on a chart, and the traditions are spot on. You can virtually keep your canoe to the left of the setting sun during those months and you'll get to the Kermadecs, and from there you'll have no trouble finding New Zealand.'

Hec's research into traditional stories didn't end there. He remembered hearing about the arrival of the Aotea canoe, and realised that he could work out roughly the time of year the migrations occurred from the story: 'The tradition recalled that when the Aotea approached the coastline her crew saw pōhutukawa trees in bloom, and, thinking the flowers were birds, they threw their sacred red-feather headgear into the ocean. Now I don't know if they actually threw their headgear away, but what the story tells us is that the Aotea arrived in the summer months, possibly in November or December, when the pōhutukawa flower is out.'

With that knowledge under his belt, Hec began to take note of when the local pōhutukawa trees flowered. The second year in which he recorded these dates, the trees bloomed two weeks later than they had the previous year, and two years after that there was an even bigger difference, of six weeks. While that in itself didn't prove anything, what did catch Hec's attention was that that particular summer was a poor season for sailing. Hec's research had uncovered a way of predicting seasonal weather patterns – at least in a general sense – by studying the natural surroundings: something his ancestors had mastered during the centuries they had lived in the Pacific.

Hec's research gave him the confidence to look to nature as a reliable guide and to use tribal traditions as a valuable source of information: something Nainoa would later acknowledge he had always had trouble coming to terms with. 'Hector's navigation is basically the same as mine, because ultimately it comes from Mau, but the main difference between us is that Hector doesn't hesitate to rely on nature. Reading the ocean and believing in it and trusting it is really a difficult skill, but Hector has always been very assured at it. Hector is a bridge-builder, right: he builds many bridges. One of those bridges is the confidence and belief in the ancestors, which is sometimes very difficult for me because I am so dislocated and disconnected from my own ancestors. I'd look at something and say it doesn't make sense mathematically, so it isn't going to work; then I'd go into a spiral and end up not trusting the very signs I was looking at. But Hector has no fear. He's at peace with the ocean. He's connected in a very deep way.'

While it's easy to jump to the conclusion that Hec is a natural navigator, in reality he had to work as much as the next man at the art. Hec explains that he was able to pick up the basic skills quickly only because he was able to put aside 21st-century knowledge and confidently use the same signs that his ancestors had relied on: 'From my experience, if you want to be a navigator, you need to know the habits of the sun, the moon and the stars, as well as being mindful of whatever clues the ocean itself can give you. It's much easier for me to use the swell, sun and stars when it comes to navigation than using complex calculations, even though I'm confident doing so. For instance, keeping on track once you are under way isn't actually too difficult if you trust yourself. Before you go, you choose the stars best positioned in the sky to guide you for that particular voyage, and then align them with your intended course. Typically you need to know about six or seven stars, and they can be fairly well spread out. If you're using a star whose position is 90 degrees to your course, all you have to do is make sure that when that star rises it is 90 degrees to the canoe – and you're okay. Then you factor in a back-up in case of total cloud cover. We usually align our course with the ocean swell, although there can be as many as four swells of varying strength coming through from different directions at any time. In those instances we normally use the most distinctive one.'

One of the skills Hec set about teaching himself early on was to judge how fast the waka was sailing: a skill any navigator relying on dead reckoning (keeping a mental track of the canoe's progress) needs to master. Hec: 'We had gotten hell from the media about the towing in '92, so we decided to sail around the North Island without a support boat in 1993–94 to demonstrate that Te Aurere was a capable vessel.' During this voyage, Hec practised estimating the waka's speed by having a crew member drop an object next to the splashboard and timing how long it took for it to reach the rear of the platform. He explains: 'If it took one second from front to back we were doing 21 knots; if it took two seconds we were doing 10.5

knots; three seconds 7 knots, and so on. As a rough guide, it works pretty well.'

Hec's ability as a navigator was later formally acknowledged in March 2008, when a group including Hec, Jack Thatcher, Piripi Evans and Tua Pittman from the Cook Islands was capped in a pwo ceremony on Mau Piailug's home island of Satawal. Hec: 'When we went over to Satawal, Mau was largely bedridden, but oh gosh, we were so glad to see one another. He had talked about his island while staying with me back in 1992, so I was keen to visit, and when we learnt he was unwell and wanted us to go over for the capping we got there as soon as possible.'

Stephen Thomas, an American who spent time studying traditional navigation from Mau in the 1980s, explains the significance of the pwo ceremony: 'In former times, one could not guide a canoe without receiving the power of Anumwerici, the spirit of navigation, in the sacred pwo ceremony. The most important event in a young navigator's life, it not only marked his passage into manhood, but also gained him entrance to a select and privileged class and gave him the right to learn secret, mystical, navigational lore.'[1] The pwo ceremony is said to date back many hundreds of years. Preparation typically begins the day before the ritual, when local men dig a shallow firepit on the beach. At the centre of the pit they stand a short log, which represents the power for the navigators. Then, before the fire is lit, one of the island's initiated navigators adds two sorts of coral to the pit: a hard coral, which represents the mental and physical toughness of the navigator, and what is known as a stinging coral, which signifies the power of the navigator's words. Later, once the fire has died down, a number of breadfruit are baked in the still-hot embers then pounded into a thick paste. The breadfruit is then put aside, along with a quantity of taro that has also been prepared specifically for the ceremony.

On the day of the ceremony, Hec and his companions were led to an open-walled canoe house, where Mau waited for them. Like the men following him, Hec entered the structure bare-chested, wearing a red lava-lava, a headband of colourful flowers and an intricately woven lei. His chest and back had been covered in a fine layer of yellow turmeric, and orange marks pointed to where his forehead and cheeks had been rubbed with a mixture containing a sacred medicine. Despite being severely weakened by his illness, Mau sat unaided in his chair, and commenced the ceremony by touching each navigator on the shoulder with a strand from the rib of a coconut frond. He then split each strand down the middle and placed one over each man's head. Next, each of the navigators was given three coconuts. As Hec explains: 'We had three tasks to complete. I can't reveal what we had to do with the first coconut, but I had to drink the second in one hit, and after the third was broken open I had to eat the flesh. All the while, Mau was watching us and reciting karakia, and Nainoa was helping us by explaining what we had to do. Later on, we were each given a sacred bracelet adorned with feathers and two stones. The bracelets were the physical symbol that showed we had reached the level of pwo, that we had become master navigators.' Finally, the newly graduated master navigators were fed the breadfruit and taro that had been prepared the previous day.

Receiving pwo from Mau was a fitting honour for the group; especially so for Hec, as Nainoa explains: 'Mau gave pwo to us, not because we are great navigators, but because we need to be the link between him and coming generations. We are really supposed to be teachers, and Hector is every bit the teacher. He has been a mentor and kapuna [elder] to many, and if you ask him he is always there for you. He is like the staff that you lean on when you need strength, and he is the standard and measurement of both commitment and values.'

Hec's pwo ceremony was the last that Mau presided over. After a long struggle with diabetes, Mau died at his home in July 2010.

But the pwo ceremony was still in the future. There was still a lot of water to flow under Te Aurere's hulls before Hec, Piripi and Jack would be anointed as navigators, including on the epic Na'ohana Holo Moana voyage through Polynesia: the final test for each of the navigators who had trained with Nainoa. The voyage would see apprentice navigators from Hawai'i, Tahiti, the Cook Islands and Aotearoa guide their waka across 2,400 miles of open ocean from the Marquesas to Hawai'i, along an ancient sea path remembered in Hawaiian traditions.

Te Aurere's part in the voyage began with a visit to Taputapuatea Marae on Ra'iatea Island (Rangiātea), where Hec and his crew would play a leading role in the lifting of a centuries-old curse.

Notes

[1] Thomas, S. *The Last Navigator*. London: Hutchinson, 1987, p. 11.

13

SAILING TE-MOANA-NUI-A-KIWA

In late 1994 Hec travelled to Rarotonga for a meeting to discuss the upcoming Nā 'Ohana Holo Moana voyage. It was scheduled to be sailed in April of the following year, and Nainoa had invited representatives from all of the participating waka to go over the proposed sail plans and discuss safety protocols and other related issues. During a break in the meeting, an elder from the island of Ra'iatea approached Hec and took him aside. He wanted Hec to consider lifting a curse that had been placed on one of their marae nearly seven centuries earlier. Hec was intrigued. He had heard the name Rangiātea in Māori traditions; he asked the elder to continue. According to the story passed down on Ra'iatea, selected tohunga from throughout Polynesia would regularly meet at Taputapuatea Marae to discuss navigation. During one of these gatherings, a crew member from Aotearoa became involved with a local woman, and was killed by the woman's husband for his troubles. Incensed by the murder, the Māori contingent departed Ra'iatea, placing a curse on both the island and a sacred pass in the reef called Te Avamo'a as they left. For the elder, the return of a Māori voyaging canoe was the perfect opportunity to revisit and remove the curse.

'I agreed to help them as soon as he finished telling me the story,' recalls Hec, 'but when I got back to my room I started to panic a little bit and thought, Holy hell. What have I agreed to? That's when I remembered some advice that John Rangihau had once passed on to me: "If you ever have a problem and you are not sure, just talk it out. Your ancestors will guide you – they're never far away." So that's what I did. Sitting alone in my room, I asked myself why I had built Te Aurere: I built it because my ancestor Tūmoana had sailed back to his Pacific homeland and I wanted to replicate his voyage, so that part was all right. The 1992 voyage had also been about going back to find our relations in the islands. Once again I was okay with that. And although way back then the tohunga said they would never return to Taputapuatea, the thing that came to me was to let bygones be bygones and to start over. So thankfully in the end I was fine with my decision.'

Back home, Hec decided he needed expert help for the curse-lifting ceremony, and he sought out Te Ao Pehi Kara, a renowned tohunga and spokesman for the Māori Queen. Hec had first met Kara through Hilda's involvement with the Kōhanga Reo movement, and their paths had crossed again when Kara had spoken on behalf of the Māori Queen on Te Aurere's arrival at Rarotonga in 1992. 'Te Ao Pehi didn't hesitate when I asked him if he wanted to get involved. In fact I'd say he jumped at the opportunity,' recalls Hec. Kara would prove to be the perfect addition to Hec's group, bringing with him both a knowledge of ancient karakia and a more than passing interest in canoes and star navigation.

Taputapuatea Marae had already seen at least one famous Māori walk upon its sacred stones during the twentieth century, when the ethnologist Te Rangi Hīroa (Sir Peter Buck) stopped in on the island briefly in 1929. Buck later recorded his impressions of the sacred site in his book *Vikings of the Sunrise*:

> Taputapu-atea stands on a low, wide cape bounded on either side by beautiful bays. The court of the temple was overgrown with weeds, but the altar (ahu), 141 feet long by 25 feet wide, bore witness to past grandeur. The stone platform was walled with huge slabs of coral limestone imbedded in the earth, and the enclosure was filled in with loose rock, through which, formerly, skulls were scattered or piled in recesses until the people had to conceal them elsewhere from the acquisitive fingers of foreign vandals. Some of the slabs rose twelve feet above the ground: some had fallen, revealing an inner row of lower wall slabs which showed that a larger platform had been built around and above a smaller structure. Thus modern decay revealed the evidence of previous growth whereby the first temple of Feoro had become Vai'otaha and finally had risen in size and importance to become the international marae of Taputapu-atea. Near the temple was an upright stone pillar, nine feet high, termed the White-rock-of-investiture (Te Papa-tea-ia-ruea). Here the head of the royal line of Opoa, girdled with a red feather belt and seated on his wooden seat of honour, was raised to the top of the pillar as part of the ceremony of investiture. Close to the beach was another marae on

> which the human sacrifices brought by canoe were laid to await their turn in the temple ritual of Taputapu-atea.

Buck finished the chapter by noting that he was particularly saddened by the state of the marae during his visit, and the loss of the marae's 'spirit'. 'The gods,' he remarked, 'had long ago departed.'

With sailing plans for the upcoming voyage having been settled during the meeting in Rarotonga and Te Ao Pehi confirmed for the tapu-lifting ceremony, Hec went about finalising arrangements for Te Aurere's expedition. Faced with the prospect of the waka's longest voyage yet and struggling to meet mounting costs (as well as being conscious that the majority of his crew were limited in the amount of leave they could take), Hec had Te Aurere shipped directly to Tahiti, rather than spend precious time and finances sailing her up. Old hands Stanley Conrad, Jack Thatcher, Piripi Evans and Martin Bercic were back, and this time Hec would also take his place upon the waka. There were also a number of new faces joining them, including Tūrakuraku (Lux) Kereopa, Dean Waharoa, Hori Ahlers, Charlie Wilson, Chris Irwin, Pohe Luttenberger, Paul Stanley, Frank Waitai and two women, Terissa Busby and Hiria Rutene.

Despite Hec's meticulous planning, the arrival of Te Aurere didn't go as smoothly as hoped. When the crew arrived in Pape'ete to take possession of the waka, they discovered that the French authorities had impounded her, after the freight forwarding company had miscalculated the fees. Hec had little money in the kitty to meet the unexpected bill, meaning that Te Aurere's participation in the tapu- ifting ceremony at Taputapuatea Marae was now in serious jeopardy. To add to Hec's woes, he quickly found that no amount of negotiating would see the vessel released without the full outstanding payment being taken care of. Hec was in a difficult position, but fortune was about to shine on him once more. Somehow word of his plight got out into the local community, and a generous donor stepped forward at the eleventh hour. The gesture saved a lot of embarrassment for Hec, and quite possibly Te Aurere's future.

While the crew waited for the payment to be processed, they kept themselves busy by helping the two Tahitian crews prepare their canoes. Karim Cowan, one of Nainoa's former students and a good friend of many of the Kiwis, was in a desperate but ultimately unsuccessful race to ready his waka 'Aa Kahiki Nui for the voyage. The other group, sponsored by the Tahitian Government, was rebuilding Hawaiki-nui, Matahi Brightwell's canoe, which had sailed from Tahiti to Aotearoa in late 1985. Marty Bercic describes the state of the waka, which had by then been renamed Tahiti Nui: 'They had stripped everything off the hulls so that they could add more height to them. The original hulls were about 6 feet high (1.8 metres), and they built another 2 feet (60 centimetres) on top of that. It certainly looked impressive, but it wasn't practical. When Hec and the Hawaiians came around and had a look at her they wondered how the crew were going to be able to use the steering paddles effectively when they took her out to sea as the deck was so high above the water.'

When the authorities finally released Te Aurere, the crew got to work readying her for the trip to Ra'iatea, under Stanley Conrad's critical eye. The hulls, mast and decking were inspected for any damage sustained during shipping, and every inch of the lashing was checked and rechecked. Stores for the short trip were loaded aboard the vessel, and special care was taken to ensure the weight was shared equally between the two hulls and balanced front and back.

The 110-mile cruise was the perfect shakedown for the crew before they faced the rigours of true deep-water voyaging. It was also a major confidence-builder for Jack Thatcher, who had struggled earlier that year during his last sail with the Hawaiians. 'At one point while we were out training with Nainoa he asked me to tell him the direction we were sailing and to explain how I'd come to my conclusion. Well, I answered him, but without a lot of conviction, so he asked if I was sure. To be honest I wasn't 100 percent sure, and I ended up changing my answer. Then he asked me again if I was sure about my second answer. By that stage I was pretty rattled and after I reassessed one more time, I came back to my original answer. Once again Nainoa asked if I was sure, which completely unsettled me, and I replied rather dejectedly that no, I wasn't sure. When we got back on land Nainoa took me aside and told me that he was worried that I wasn't ready for the upcoming voyage to Hawai'i. Of course I was pretty upset with myself at the time, but in the end that reality check made me more determined than ever to prepare myself for the voyage.'

In the months that followed, Jack refocused his study and regained his confidence, and by the time Te Aurere had arrived off Ra'iatea in the predawn darkness of 18 March

1995, he was ready. This day, however, belonged to Hec and Te Ao Pehi Kara. With Hōkūle'a, Hawai'iloa, Tahiti Nui and the Rarotongan waka Takitumu sitting astern of Te Aurere, the two men waited for the first rays of the sun to reach out across the ocean, before Hec gave the order for his crew to manoeuvre their waka through Te Avamo'a pass. Once they had reached the lagoon inside the reef, Te Ao Pehi, thickset, bespectacled and with greying hair, began to recite his karakia:

Tiwha tiwha te Pō, Tiwha tiwha te Ao
He whare i mahue kau e he whare i mahue kau e
Ka whatinga ake te kura o te marama
Ka pahuka mai te moana i ngā tai e ngunguru nei
Tēnei ko te toka ki a tātou kua hinga rātou kua hinga
Kua takoto i te ringa kaha o Aitua

Tēnei te nihinihi tēnei te nana
Tēnei te wā hikitia ngā tapu
O runga i tēnei kokoru ki runga
i ō tatou mātua tūpuna
E tangi ake nei te ngākau
Turuturu o whiti whakamau kia tina
Tina! Hui e, taiki e.

Dark is the night, gloomy the day
The house is left desolate and abandoned
A fragment of the moon is torn away
The sea froths as the waves rush ashore
This is our rock, the rock is left to us

For they have passed on
Laid low by the strong hand of death
This is the neap tide and the raging tide
It is time to remove the tapu
From this bay onto our ancestors
The heart is moved
So let it be for all time
We are united![1]

It was an unforgettable experience for all involved. Hec: 'It was so beautiful. I was in a trance as Te Ao Pehi spoke, and boy oh boy – I've never felt like that in my whole life. I could feel the canoe being surrounded by our ancestors.'

By the time Te Ao Pehi had completed his incantations and lifted the curse, outrigger canoes had come alongside Te Aurere to carry the crew across the lagoon to the marae. Once ashore, each man was draped in fragrant lei and led past tattooed drummers to a sheltered corner of the marae. Here they waited under towering coconut trees until each of their fellow crews had entered the marae. Marty Bercic recalls that even before the last of the five crews had arrived, the mounting heat began to take its toll on those assembled for the historic ceremony: 'They have flat rocks like paving stones on their marae, rather than the grass we have back home, and the stones got hotter and hotter as the sun got higher and higher. We were lucky though. Because we were first in we got put into a corner where there was a little bit of shade, but we were soon watching other crews lose people to the heat – they would just drop.'

Despite the soaring temperatures, some 1500 spectators and officials were on hand to listen to numerous emotionally charged speeches and to witness each of the visiting crews place a stone mauri on the marae as a symbol of renewed friendship.

After the ceremony, the small fleet of canoes sailed to the nearby isle of Tahaa for a feast, and in the morning a number of other invited guests climbed aboard Te Aurere for the voyage back to Pape'ete. For Te Ao Pehi it was an opportunity to discuss star names and traditional navigation with Jack Thatcher. Marty again: 'Te Ao Pehi had been brought up in the old wānanga where they were taught star patterns. He knew the star names backwards, and he knew a number of chants that listed stars, but he had never been able to figure out their true context. Te Ao Pehi and Jack spent hours together talking about stars. Te Ao Pehi would recite a karakia or chant, and Jack would listen out for familiar names and try to interpret the meaning: this star, that star, that star, and that star – and if you follow that line of stars it goes in that direction, and so that's your star path. So for Te Ao Pehi the trip helped him close a circle of knowledge. They were no longer just a collection of names for him.'

When the fleet arrived back in Pape'ete, the crews took on fresh supplies before heading to their departure point at Tautira Bay (Cook's Anchorage), on the south-east coast of Tahiti's Taiarapu Peninsula. There they dropped anchor and waited for favourable winds. This became the setting for what would become a legendary moment in the history of Te Aurere, as Marty elaborates: 'We had a couple of girls hanging around while we were in Pape'ete, and when they heard we were about to leave, one of them asked Hector if they could sail around to Tautira with us. He told her that he wasn't the captain and that she would have to ask Stanley. Well, because Hec didn't say no, it kind of meant that it was okay for them to come along, so Stanley gave the thumbs up and they jumped on board. When we got to Tautira we were a little surprised to see flashing lights going off and gendarmes everywhere and this poor Tahitian man crying in the background. He eventually came on board with the gendarmes and said in broken English, "These Māoris have stolen my daughter!" That's when one of the gendarmes demanded to know who the captain was. Stanley looked at Hector and Hector looked at Stanley, and Hector goes, "Him!" Fortunately we had a Tahitian on board who translated and sorted it out for us. It turns out the girls had been taking time off school for a couple of weeks, and they weren't quite as old as they told us. It was pretty innocent stuff, but the poor dad had thought we were taking the girls to the Marquesas with us. As it happens one of our Hawaiian mates had come down to make sure we docked okay, and he was pissing himself with laughter at the thought that Stanley might get arrested, so by the time we got out to where the rest of the canoes were anchored they were ready for us. Of course they had all learnt the reason why our tūpuna had been murdered at Taputapuatea all those years ago, and they couldn't help themselves: "Bloody Māoris trying to steal women again!"'

The departure for Nuku Hiva, 750 miles to the north-east, was a low-key affair. The crews of Hawai'iloa, Te Aurere, Takitumu, the second Cook Island waka Te Au o Tonga and the recently finished Hawaiian canoe Makali'i raised their sails on 5 April. Hōkūle'a wouldn't depart until the sixth, while Tahiti Nui, still hampered by difficulties relating to steering, wouldn't leave Pape'ete for another day or so; the badly redesigned canoe would remain under navy escort for the duration of her voyage.

Once under way, the canoes were soon forced to hook up to their support boats to ensure they arrived in the Marquesas in good time. It wasn't the ideal start to their adventure, but as Ben Finney pointed out in his book *Sailing in the Wake of the Ancestors*, the leg to the Marquesas 'was simply to position the canoes for the all-important crossing to Hawai'i, not to investigate how to sail from Tahiti to Marquesas'. Finney also noted that 'the towing was boring and distasteful … we did not have enough time to wait for ideal winds or tack laboriously into the light headwinds plaguing us'.

The trip remained uneventful for the crew of Te Aurere until, just a few days out from their arrival in the Marquesas, word came through that Hec's elder brother Hugh had succumbed to throat cancer. Hec, trapped on a waka half an ocean away, was deeply shaken by the news. The best he could do was offer a prayer, and dedicate the upcoming leg in Hugh's memory.

Unsurprisingly, the final days of the passage were largely a sombre affair, although there was one isolated moment of humour, when the crew spotted a rain-laden cloud formation sweeping towards them a couple of hours out from the Marquesas. Marty: 'We always made sure we had a good wash before we arrived at an island, so when we saw the rain cloud coming our way we all grabbed our soap and lathered up, but just as we finished soaping up every spot we could think of the bloody rain stopped, leaving us standing around with soap drying all over and looking like a bunch of Aborigines!'

Thanks to the powerful engines of their support boat the *Kama Hele*, Hawai'iloa and Te Aurere reached Nuku Hiva a day and a half before the next waka, on 12 April. Because officials on the island were eager to see the entire fleet enter Taiohae Bay together for the formal welcome, the two canoes were sent to an alternative anchorage off the small township of Taipivai. There, several of Te Aurere's crew decided to swim to shore to explore. It was a painful decision: unbeknown to the crew, they were anchored above a bed of vana – a kina-like sea urchin with long spikes terminating in a barbed hook and an irritating sting. Several pairs of feet, including Hec's, benefited from a visit by the *Kama Hele*'s medical officer. Marty observed the whole performance: 'I hadn't jumped into the bay, so for me it was quite funny watching the doctor at work. He was trying to help them, but you could see it was bloody well hurting them as he dug the spikes out. I remember watching Hector's fist tightening as the doctor dug in. It was hard not to chuckle, but of course the boss wasn't a happy camper.'

When word reached officials that Hōkūle'a, Makali'i and Te Au o Tonga were closing in on Nuku Hiva, it was decided that the official welcoming ceremony would take place on Good Friday, 14 April, despite confirmation that Tahiti Nui and Takitumu wouldn't arrive in time. Once again, a magnificent welcome awaited the crews; it seemed as if every inhabitant of the island had turned out for the occasion. Conch shells called the waka into the bay, and continued to signal as the crews came ashore. The ceremony, held on a grassy reserve above the beach, saw forty spear-wielding Marquesan warriors and a similar number of women put on a memorable performance for the crews. Marty: 'We were really pōhara when we went over, and we only had enough money to fly our crew in and out and feed them. By comparison, the Tahitians were funded by their government, and the Rarotongans were very well supported, as were the Hawaiians. When it came time for the speeches, we soon realised that all of the other crews had brought these lavish gifts to present to the mayor. We hadn't actually thought about gifts, and we were still scratching our heads wondering what the hell we were going to do when it came time for Hector's speech. He started with the usual formalities and then said, "Well, we don't really have too much. We only came with ourselves and whatnot, so I'm going to give you the shirt off my back." And he took off his shirt and handed it to the mayor. Fortunately the mayor really appreciated the gesture, and from that moment on they were like two long-lost brothers.'

Two days later Hec and his crew were among those who made their way down to the beach to welcome Tahiti Nui and Takitumu. Stanley: 'There was quite a swell rolling in to the bay, and the breakers were crashing from about 100 metres off shore – so the two canoes anchored well out and the locals sent out a longboat to bring in the crews. I guess everyone wanted to get to shore on the first boat, because it had about twenty people on board when it should have had a maximum of about ten. We were just above the beach eating ice creams as the longboat came in, and we could make out a guy riding the front of the boat looking like Captain Jack Sparrow. He was wearing jackboots and a *Pirates of the Caribbean*-type of hat with big feathers, along with a knife or something in his belt. As they got closer to shore he put his foot up on the front of the longboat and was standing there with his hands on his hips, posing like an explorer discovering the New World. As you can imagine it was quite a sight. Well, they were flying in – that is until they ran out of water. You could see the concertina effect from the back of the longboat – boom, boom, boom, boom – and then the guy got jettisoned out the front. He had been so serious as well … so you can imagine what it was like for a group of Māori boys. It was bloody hilarious.'

In the days before their departure for Hawai'i, the waka were sailed to outlying islands in the Marquesas group to allow the crews to share their passion for voyaging. During Te Aurere's visit to 'Ua Pou, a small island about 50 kilometres south of Nuku Hiva, the crew were struck by the closeness of the inhabitants' dialect to the New Zealand Māori language. The language of Nuku Hiva had been vaguely similar to Māori, but there was no mistaking the meaning of the speeches when they arrived at 'Ua Pou. If any of the crew had doubted how strong the ties between Māori and their Pacific neighbours were, those reservations were surely dispelled by this visit. That appreciation was only strengthened when the crew's haka was challenged later during their stay by a couple of elderly natives. Marty: 'During one of the welcomes we got up and supported Hector after he completed his speech. While we were doing the haka a couple of old guys, both probably well into their sixties, started challenging us by doing their version of the haka. It imitated the movements and sound of wild boars, like a pig rutting through the woods. It had a real stomping type of action, and by the time they had finished they were right up in our faces. Hector said that he had only seen it done like that once before in similar circumstances, back when he was a boy. He said it was a huge honour to have the haka done back at us, especially by elders. He was chuffed.'

As far as long-distance voyages within Polynesia go, the leg from the Marquesas to Hawai'i is generally considered a fairly straightforward route to navigate using traditional methods. While it obviously takes skill to guide a waka across any expanse of ocean, the winds are usually favourable for the passage north, and often the only test a navigator will endure is the Intertropical Convergence Zone, or the doldrums, as it is commonly known. Navigators are aided by the fact that the Marquesas are situated to the east of Hawai'i's longitude: as long as a navigator keeps his waka to the east of Hawai'i's position as he makes his way north, he can rely on the north-easterly trade winds to push his craft downwind when it arrives at Hawai'i's latitude. As Jack confirms, navigating the voyage wasn't overly onerous: 'Because of Hawai'i's position relative to Nuku Hiva we had nothing to worry about as long as we stayed to the east of Hawai'i. Even if we were a hundred miles or more to the east of the island and couldn't physically see it, we could judge our latitude by the height of the Southern Cross above the horizon. That was the sign we used to tell us when to turn west.'

For this leg of the journey, the navigators divided the voyage into four sections. In the first, Te Aurere would sail due north from Nuku Hiva (located 9 degrees south of the equator) to the bottom of the doldrums (3 degrees north of the equator): a total of 720 miles. Sailing at an average of 4 knots, the leg would take seven and a half days. The second section ran from 3 degrees north of the equator to 9 degrees north of the equator, and covered the latitudes the doldrums inhabited. An estimated average speed of 2.5 knots would see the vessel cover the 360 miles of the leg in six days, and again the sail plan required the navigators to head due north. The third and longest section extended from 9 degrees north of the equator to 20 degrees, 30 minutes north of the equator. With fresher winds expected during this 760-mile leg, the estimated speed was increased to 5 knots, meaning that if everything went to plan, the canoe would arrive to the east of Hawai'i a little over six days after leaving the doldrums. Having reached the latitude of Hawai'i, the crew would then simply turn their vessel due west for the final 370-mile section. Then, like the navigators of old, Jack and Piripi would target a 240-mile block consisting of several of the major Hawaiian islands, rather than any single point along the coasts. Once again the navigators would calculate their progress on an estimated speed of 5 knots for the final section, which would see Te Aurere nearing land some three and a half days after turning west. Finally, once a coast was sighted and their exact position confirmed, the navigators would adjust their course and sail for a specific destination, in much the same way as Stanley Conrad had guided Hōkūle'a to the Bay of Islands after her crew had sighted Northland in 1985.

Te Aurere was the first of three waka to leave Taiohae Bay on 19 April; it was another emotional farewell for Hec: 'As always, it was hard to say goodbye. I jumped on Te Aurere to do the karakia for them, and only hopped off at the last minute when they were about to pull up the anchor. As usual I broke down and started blubbering like a baby – it's just the way it is.'

Hawai'iloa followed Te Aurere's departure two hours later, and Makali'i raised her anchor a further two hours after her. Three more waka, Te Au o Tonga, Takitumu and Hōkūle'a, each set sail the following day, also departing at two-hourly intervals. These staggered departures allowed the navigators time to commence their voyage without undue influence from other waka.

Unhappily for the Tahitians, Tahiti Nui was withdrawn from the fleet at the last minute, joining 'Aa Kahiki Nui as a non-starter. The realisation that neither of Tahiti's waka would participate in the voyage was disappointing, but inevitable. 'Aa Kahiki Nui was still back in Pape'ete, having failed to get clearance for the sail across to the Marquesas, and Tahiti Nui, as predicted, was proving impossible to manoeuvre.

Once under way, Jack and Piripi settled into their navigation duties under favourable conditions: 8–15-knot winds were coming from the easterly quarter, along with a current that they estimated would push the canoes 12 miles to the west each day. Fair sailing continued into the second day, and was only marginally interrupted by the arrival of squalls. By evening the associated cloud cover had cleared enough to allow the navigators to guide their craft by the stars, as swells from the east and north-east slipped under Te Aurere's twin hulls.

As Te Aurere neared the equator a few days later, the crew witnessed one of nature's more awe-inspiring sights: a pod of perhaps one hundred dolphins surrounded the vessel and proceeded to entertain the crew. Captivated by the power and grace of the dolphins, many on board considered that the dolphins were guardians sent to lead the waka across the equator. If that was the case, it was perhaps the dolphins that also ensured settled sailing conditions remained until Te Aurere entered the doldrums on 27 April, when heavy cloud cover arrived.

Despite being unable to view the stars, Te Aurere's navigators were able to rely on 4–5-foot swells, generated by the trade winds, to help with their wayfinding. By ensuring that the direction the canoe sailed remained constant in relation to the angle of the swells rolling under their hulls, they could be sure that they remained on course. Then, as if to compensate for the arrival of the clouds, strong north-easterlies held as Te Aurere raced through the doldrums, taking just over half of the six days they had allowed in their sail plan to pass through the zone. Such was her progress that by the time Te Aurere had departed the doldrums she had lost contact with her support boat *On the Way*, and it was several hours before the two vessels were reunited. Jack: 'Once we were back together, we changed our course to about 22 degrees west of north. As expected, the winds changed from easterlies to north-easterlies as we climbed higher, and they grew in strength to 15–20 knots, which allowed us to average around 5 knots and cover 120 miles a day.'

With sails straining and tropical waters surging between her hulls, Te Aurere sped north, her two navigators keeping an anxious eye on the heavens, each hoping that the largely clear skies would hold. Both men had spent a considerable amount of time training in Hawaiian waters during the preceding three years, and both were familiar with the night sky viewed from Hawai'i, including the Southern Cross's place in the cosmos. Jack: 'You know you are at Hawai'i's latitude when you see the Southern Cross standing upright, and its height above the horizon is the same as it is tall. Once we saw the Southern Cross in that position, all we had to do was turn west. It was that simple. So as long as we didn't have total cloud cover, Piripi and I were never going to miss the Hawaiian Island chain.' And they didn't. As the Southern Cross inched its way into position, the navigators gave the word to turn westward. Hawai'i sat downwind of them, and for all intents and purposes they were through the toughest sections of their voyage.

The crew's arrival in Hawai'i wasn't quite what they had envisaged, though: the fleet was waylaid by the discovery of nono, a tiny sandfly with an aggressive attitude, aboard a number of the waka. Nainoa, who was in regular contact with all the vessels to record each navigator's estimate of their progress, ordered the fleet to lower sails while he contacted officials in Hawai'i; he knew that the nono were a serious threat to both Hawai'i's environment and her tourist industry. When instructions came through from Hawai'i, they were explicit: each crew was to throw all of their fresh food, plants and other materials that might harbour the insects overboard, and then to scrub down their vessels while they waited for canisters of insecticide to be air-dropped by the United States Coast Guard. Once the canoes had been sprayed inside and out, the crews were to heave-to for a further twenty-four hours before proceeding to Hilo, where each canoe would recieve a comprehensive spraying in huge fumigation tents.

It was a frustrating delay, but one that barely dampened the celebratory mood onboard Te Aurere when she arrived in Hilo on 7 May. Her navigators had succeeded in guiding their waka to her destination, and, thanks in part to a dedicated crew, had managed to adhere remarkably closely to their sail plan.

In all, Te Aurere's voyage had lasted eighteen days – five less than planned – and she had once again proven her sailing ability under a variety of conditions. As Hec stood among the welcoming crowds watching Te Aurere tie up, he couldn't help but think of Sir James Henare and his speech that had so eloquently challenged Māori to build a voyaging canoe of their own and sail it to Hawai'i. It had taken him ten years to meet Sir James's challenge, and he was proud of his waka and her crew.

As is usually the case with longer voyages, the make-up of Te Aurere's crew changed from leg to leg. A number of those who had sailed up to Hawai'i needed to return to New Zealand for work commitments, including Piripi Evans and Stanley Conrad. Both had originally intended to sail as far as Rarotonga, but the various delays had eaten into their leave allocations. With their departure, Hec would take over Te Aurere's captaincy himself, and Jack would be afforded the opportunity to test his skills as the sole navigator. Another to join the crew was Mau Piailug's son Sesario, who was himself an apprentice navigator and who had just completed the voyage up from the Marquesas aboard the Hōkūle'a.

Their departure on 1 June preceded the worst of the hurricane season by some weeks, but nonetheless allowed the crew to take advantage of strengthening winds. The favourable conditions should have seen Te Aurere cover a considerable distance during the first week, but instead that week was memorable for the frustration the crew felt with yet another unreliable support boat. Just days out from port, the *Potzalana*'s watermaker broke, necessitating the transfer of five 20-litre containers of water from Te Aurere, and then her motor started to play up. As if that wasn't enough, the two boats were not well matched in sailing performance either. Hec: 'We had to wait for the support boat quite a lot. She would get ahead of us in light winds, but when the winds were strong we would leave her behind, so we had to regularly reduce sail. At one point we had to wait a day and a half for the boat to catch up to us. The voyage wasn't all bad though: it was actually one of the best trips for fishing. We only had to fish for about ten minutes on daybreak to catch all that we needed. We were catching mahimahi and different types of tuna. We even hooked a marlin. We dried some, boiled some, made sashimi, and fried some.' They also got to witness the spectacular arrival of Matariki (the Pleiades) in the night sky on 11 June.

From Jack's viewpoint, the canoe's progress was pleasing. She was making good time before fresh winds, and he felt confident that he was following his sail plan closely – only he wasn't. By the time Te Aurere had reached the doldrums, she was already considerably off course, and a prolonged period while the canoe sat becalmed in changable conditions only exacerbated the situation. 'I had a real big cock-up on the trip. It was initially caused by my need to prove myself, but ultimately I overlooked the signs that would have put me back on track.' The leg had started off well enough, but Jack's desire to live by Nainoa's mantra that a navigator has to know where he is twenty-four hours a day eventually began to take its toll: 'I was trying to do everything the hard way. I'd sleep for half-hour periods, maybe snatching three or four hours' sleep total each day. I remember during one thirty-six-hour period I got no sleep at all because I was micro-managing the crew, whereas you need to have a lot of trust in the people you are sailing with. There were actually four really experienced crew onboard who knew how to run the waka in any conditions, and all I should have been doing was monitoring what they were doing – and if they went off course, kei te pai. As long as I knew they went off course it didn't matter – I could factor it in to my calculations.

'The main problem was that I didn't pick up that we were drifting west of our course line. It wasn't until Mau's son Sesario came up to me and pointed out a small flock of birds skimming across the ocean that I had an inkling that I might be off course. I had actually been watching them and thinking, No, that can't be right. If those birds are here then that would mean we are within 100 miles of an island, maybe even closer, and I had already calculated we should be at least 200 miles from Christmas Island. The evidence was there, but the brain was telling me to discount it.' There was no doubt in Sesario's mind that they were looking at land-based birds: a conclusion that Jack would eventually arrive at as well. 'They were acting exactly how land-based birds behave while out fishing,' Jack explains: 'flying close to the water and criss-crossing the ocean while searching for food, and then spending time sitting on the water. They'll feed and rest, feed and rest, and just before dark they'll fly home. Those birds fly, say, 100–120 miles maximum from land. I knew that we were close to Christmas Island's latitude, so I said to Sesario, "I know it looks like those are land-based birds, but I'm not convinced. Why would they be this far out?" Well, we watched the birds and sure enough they took off at dusk, and Sesario says, "Did you see? Did you see? They flew in that direction. The island is there." And I'm going, "Oh no – you're right!"'

After a restless night, Hec took Jack aside the next morning and confirmed Sesario's observation. Hec: 'Jack was very accurate in estimating how far south we had sailed, but he was out in his west–east calculations, because he hadn't been allowing enough for the drift.' Jack continues: 'My first thought when Hec told me how far out we were was that there must be something caught on the lee board. It was a classic instance of blaming the instrument and not the person. But I soon realised that that wouldn't have caused us to go so far off course. What was making us go off course was my inability to track our progress accurately. I should have just acknowledged we were off course, instead of trying to find some other reason for it. Naturally I was a bit down, but the boys were supportive, telling me not to worry about it and that I'd soon get back on track.'

According to Robert Gable, Hec's management of Jack's miscalculation was typical of the way he operates on board. It was, Robert maintains, an extension of his everyday persona – a fact acknowledged and respected by the crew: 'Hec's a very good captain, and the crew has a lot of faith in him. There's a strong spiritual dimension that he brings to the waka through his karakia. He believes that if you do something properly, spiritually, that you'll achieve your goals, and that rubs off on the crew.' Hec was able to separate himself from his desire for a perfect voyage and allow Jack to recover from, and correct, his error. Going solo on such a demanding leg had been a steep learning curve for Jack, but one he would embrace and draw on in subsequent voyages, including the final leg from Rarotonga to Aotearoa.

Once Hec had confirmed the canoe's actual position, Jack set about guiding the vessel down past Malden and Starbuck islands and back to the course line set in the sail plan: 'After I got back on course I don't think I was more than a few miles out for the rest of the trip. I'd decided to sleep a little more and let the guys do their work, and we actually had quite a good time of it during the last ten days we were out there – although we did get becalmed again. We had hoped to call in to the Northern Cooks to watch the Rugby World Cup final which was being played in South Africa, but we got becalmed for two days about 35 miles out from Penrhyn Island. Fortunately though the guy on the radio in Rarotonga broadcast the game, so we could at least listen to it.' Te Aurere finally arrived in Rarotonga on 30 June, once again to a heroes' welcome and another celebratory feast.

Safely in Rarotonga, but with the worst of the southern winter still before them, Hec put Te Aurere in dry dock while the crew flew back to New Zealand to wait for the southern sailing season. The waka had already suffered at the hands of winter storms in 1992, and Hec was determined to time the last leg to coincide with the migration of the kūaka to Aotearoa – the traditional sign for navigators of old that the weather was settling and it was safe to sail into southern waters.

When Hec himself arrived home, he was met by some troubling news: during his absence, Hilda had been admitted to hospital. She had been feeling unwell for some months, and after visiting her GP she had been sent for a thorough check-up at Whāngārei Hospital. There, a barrage of tests confirmed her doctor's worst fears – she had cancer, and there was little they could do for her. Hilda kept the full diagnosis to herself. She was determined not to let her illness affect Hec while he was preparing to return to Rarotonga. Hec: 'I knew she was unwell, but I never dreamt she was as ill as it turned out. After I returned to Rarotonga I spoke to her every day, and I told her that I would pull out of the voyage to return home to look after her – that Jack could bring the canoe back – but she insisted that I make sure the canoe got home. So with Hilda being Hilda, that was that.'

When the crew arrived back in Rarotonga to prepare Te Aurere for the final leg of her odyssey, there were a number of replacements in their midst, including Hec's niece Terissa Busby, who would become the first woman to voyage on a waka hourua from the central Pacific to Aotearoa for several hundred years. Another was noted academic and waterman Hoturoa Kerr, who would join the crew for the return leg, as would famed author, yachtsman and adventurer David Lewis. Now in his late seventies, Lewis had written the seminal book *We, the Navigators* after sailing the Pacific in the 1960s in search of traditional navigators and Pacific wayfinding lore. On this voyage he would have the opportunity to observe a Māori navigating a voyaging canoe with consummate skill first-hand, a feat inconceivable just ten years previously. Jack: 'The leg home was probably the hardest leg I'd had to navigate up to that point, even taking into account the difficulties I had during the previous leg. We had total cloud cover for most of the voyage, and I had to rely on the swells to keep track of our progress.' Jack's main challenge was that faced by any traditional navigator who relies on this method: a swell might be useful for several days, but it will eventually fade, and if that happens while the navigator is resting, as it did during this final leg, the waka can easily go off course. 'We were using the roll of the swell under us to keep on track, but while I was sleeping, the wind that had been forming the local swell shifted – not a lot, but enough to make a difference – and we started to wander off course. Mau would have picked up on that quite easily, probably even from his bunk, but I didn't notice it until I realised that the sun wasn't where I expected it to be when I checked at midday.' Over the course of the voyage, Jack had formed a clear picture of where the sun should sit at midday. His habit of standing at the base of one of the masts as the sun reached its zenith each day meant he could easily spot any significant variation in the canoe's position.

As the days passed and the ocean temperature began to drop, Jack began searching in earnest for signs that their destination was nearing. The most likely hint would be the one that Kupe's wife had first seen centuries earlier when Matahourua was approaching Aotearoa – a bank of clouds in the distance. 'I'd studied cloud formations as part of my preparation for the voyage, so I knew to expect to see big, stationary cumulus clouds even before land was visible, and sure enough a day out from arriving we saw the fabled long white cloud. Then, a couple of hours later when the sun was going down, it started to disappear before it hit the horizon. I knew straight away we were home, because there was obviously something in front of the setting sun, and it could only be land.' Hec would later say that Jack had put on a masterclass during the leg from Rarotonga, and it had been as close to how Nainoa would have handled the conditions as you could hope to see. Jack Thatcher, he declared, had come of age as a navigator.

Te Aurere arrived home in Doubtless Bay on the morning of 30 November 1995, twenty-one days after departing Rarotonga. Her epic voyage had seen her sail just under 8000 miles. It was a triumphant return, but one that Hilda missed. Hec: 'When we got back she couldn't even make it down to the beach. I'd spoken to her every day while we were coming home, and she never once let on how sick she was. Her voice was so strong that I thought she was fine.' Hilda had tried her best to shield her husband from the truth while she continued to fight the illness, but in the end there was no hiding it. She passed away on 29 January 1996, surrounded by family and close friends in the home she had shared with Hec in Kamo East.

Unsurprisingly, given the position she had held within the communities she lived and worked in, Hilda's tangi was widely attended. It began with colleagues and acquaintances paying their respects at Taka Porowini Marae in Whāngārei, before Hilda was taken to her family's marae Te Rāwhitiroa (Te AhuAhu) at Ōhaeawai for a short period. From there, she was moved to

Aurere, where representatives from Kōhanga Reo, Te Puni Kōkiri, the National Māori Women's Welfare League and the numerous other committees that she had been involved with over the years paid their respects. Government officials including Sir Don McKinnon also travelled north for the tangi. Hilda's life had been dedicated to working for her people, and many of the speeches lavished praise upon both her life and work. During her years working for the Department of Māori Affairs, she had helped countless individuals from all walks of life, and before that she had been a founding member of the Māori Women's Welfare League, alongside Whina Cooper, Mira Szaszy and others. In her later years she had received a number of honours, including the Queen's Service Medal and the New Zealand Commonwealth Medal, which principally recognised her work for her people.

The praise amassed upon Hilda's memory was a fitting tribute to a remarkable woman, but no eulogy, no matter how heartfelt, could help ease Hec's pain. He was, for all intents and purposes, a broken man.

Notes

[1] The portions of Te Ao Pehi's karakia and his free English translation reproduced here were provided by the tohunga himself, and first appeared in Finney, B. *Sailing in the Wake of the Ancestors: Reviving Polynesian Voyaging*. Honolulu: Bishop Museum, 2003, pp. 54–5.

14

INTO THE NEW MILLENNIUM

Hec's years with Hilda had seen him accomplish a significant amount for Māori, and he would later confide that he doubts he would have been able to achieve nearly as much without her at his side. She was, he says, his backbone, believing in everything he did and supporting him unconditionally. Naturally enough her untimely passing left an intolerable vacuum in his life, and in the aftermath of her tangi Hec turned to drink, as Stanley Conrad reflects: 'Hec was at his lowest after Hilda died. He began drinking heavily, and didn't look after himself. He more or less gave up. It was a dark, dark period in his life. He just couldn't accept she had gone. He'd always imagined that he would go first.'

'He was like that for a couple of years really,' continues Pita Paraone, 'until Hilda's daughter Gina and her husband Michael moved to Aurere in December of 1998. And I take my hat off to them for that. They left a comfortable life in Whāngārei to look after Hector, and I think that's a reflection of the mana that Hector has; that you have the stepdaughter and her husband giving him the due respect that her mother would have expected her to give him.'

It's easy to underestimate the importance of Michael and Gina's contribution in the greater scheme of things. Their constant support saw Hec begin to recover. It wasn't all plain sailing though. Even at the best of times, he can be tempestuous, irritable and demanding, and those who knew him best struggled to lift the gloom that choked his world after Hilda's passing. The sailing programme that he and others had worked so hard to establish eventually deteriorated, to the point that, by 1998, training wānanga had ceased completely and Te Aurere was permanently at her mooring. Hec later admitted that he was all but ready to give up his involvement with waka; that after Hilda's death his heart was no longer in it.

That would all change, however, when he received an invitation to participate in the annual International Festival of Canoes in Hawai'i in 1999. The festival would not only present Hec with the opportunity to showcase his talents to an appreciative audience; it would also allow him to mingle and share knowledge and ideas with like-minded canoe-builders from different cultures. Carvers from all over the Pacific – Tongans, Tahitians, Cook Islanders, Inuit, Hawaiians and others – were invited to build canoes during the two-week long festival.

The festival provided an atmosphere in which Hec thrived, and he returned to it for ten consecutive years. He later cited a desire to repay the support the Hawaiians had given him as the main reason for his initial attendance. Whatever the motivation, it would prove to be just the boost he needed to rekindle his passion for waka.

On his return from the first festival in 1999, his appetite for canoes and voyaging once again whetted, Hec announced to his core supporters and crew that he was planning to take Te Aurere to New Caledonia. The 2000-mile round trip would be timed to coincide with the eighth quadrennial Festival of Pacific Arts, which was scheduled for late October 2000. Furthermore, he would be sailing Te Aurere around the North Island to prepare for the voyage. This circumnavigation would be the perfect opportunity to ease back into voyaging, tune up Te Aurere and bring through several new crew members, including Ray (Moko) Henare and Wati Forbes, who would each feature in several future voyages.

'The last time we sailed around the island was a bloody good trip, and the boys learnt some important lessons along the way,' recalls Hec. One such lesson occurred just south of Kaipara Heads, where crew inexperience saw Te Aurere lose her way. 'I'd set a course that would see us sail south, parallel with the coast, all the way down to Manukau Harbour. As the wind was coming from the land, I knew we were pretty safe and couldn't be blown ashore, so I figured it would be a good opportunity to take a short nap. Before I turned in I checked the swell, which was hitting our bow on a 45-degree angle from the west, and then I jumped up onto the top of the starboard hull, pulled a spare sail around me and drifted off to sleep with the boom directly above me. After a while I woke up – I'm not sure why, but I think I probably sensed something had changed – and when I checked the sails were on the other side of the waka. I immediately asked the steersman what was wrong, and he replied that the wind had changed. I was pretty sure that the wind couldn't have changed that much in the short time I had been asleep, so I asked him which way the swell was hitting us.' The steersman's answer, that the swell was hitting the stern, confirmed Hec's suspicion. His reply was immediate and to the point: 'Then you'd better turn this bloody thing around – we're heading north!'

It was a good lesson, and one that Hec still uses during wānanga. 'The guy in question gets really embarrassed when I bring it up, but I remind him that it's important for the others to learn from our mistake, and I know that once they hear that story they don't forget it. He was actually quite an experienced crew member at the time, but he hadn't been in a decision-making role during any of his trips, so his level of observation wasn't quite as high as it could have been.'

The remainder of the circumnavigation went to plan, and Hec began to prepare for the journey to New Caledonia. The sail plan commenced with a 528-mile leg from Mangōnui in Northland to Norfolk Island, where Te Aurere would rendezvous with the Cook Island waka Te Au o Tonga. From there the two canoes would sail the remaining 470 miles to Noumea in tandem. It promised to be a fairly straightforward voyage; Hec's only real concern was the possibility of meeting storms along the way, as the festival was scheduled for the tail end of the winter months.

Once again Te Aurere's departure was delayed, this time by last-minute complications getting her Category 1 clearance from the Maritime Safety Authority signed off: a requirement for all vessels wishing to leave coastal waters unescorted. The delay meant not only that they would miss meeting up with Te Au o Tonga at Norfolk Island but also that, for a second time, they would miss the opening ceremony of the Festival of Pacific Arts. Te Aurere's revised departure date of 12 October also resulted in a revised course, which would see the navigators – Hec, who was now well advanced in his navigation studies, and the experienced Piripi Evans – set a more direct route, first heading due north past the Tropic of Capricorn before turning west and heading for Noumea. Hec: 'The sail up wasn't too taxing, as we could rely on the Southern Cross to guide us, and as long as we kept it on our stern and made allowances for any lateral drift, we knew we were heading due north.'

When the crew sighted New Caledonia after eight days at sea they could have been forgiven for thinking that the first leg of their voyage was over, but another three frustrating days stood between the sighting and the crew standing on terra firma. As crew member Anaru Reedy recalls: 'On arriving at the south-west tip of New Caledonia, we were hit by some pretty nasty weather and we had difficulty tacking towards the entrance to Noumea. Our first attempt failed and we were driven back … and we waited till morning to have another go. We got to within a few kilometres of the entrance, but the wind changed to norwest and we were dangerously close to the reef, so Hector gave the order for us to head back south.'[1]

The next day they tried again to make port, this time sailing 60 miles offshore before tacking back to the pass, but once again their efforts were foiled. Conscious of his tiring crew and the dangerous reefs in their vicinity, Hec decided to retreat well offshore, where they could safely heave-to and wait for morning. It was a prudent decision, but an unfortunate one. As the first rays of light danced across the ocean the next morning, Hec found to his dismay that they had been driven south by unseen currents during the night, and Te Aurere now sat closer to the Isle of Pines than Noumea. Irritated beyond description, Hec decided to make for the Isle of Pines where he could employ a local guide to help them complete their journey.

Once ashore, Hec made preliminary enquiries in his search for a reliable guide, but ultimately decided that Te Aurere and her exhausted crew would be better off remaining on the island. The final three days of the voyage had taken a lot out of them; Hec explains that at that stage he simply preferred for his crew to stay among the Kunie people and rest. The experience of sailing the canoe to New Caledonia was undoubtedly the focus of the trip as far as Hec was concerned – more so than attending the festival – and for many of the crew, the interaction with the indigenous people of the island was the highlight of the trip. Anaru explains: 'The manaakitanga of the Kunie towards us was just so kind and generous. They fed us three cooked meals a day for the five days we were on the island, something that I will always treasure in my heart.'

It was another fine example of the Pacific-wide generosity that Hec and his crew encountered during their years of voyaging. Hec: 'It was wonderful staying with the Kunie people, and they were very generous towards us. Actually, up until that trip I considered the Rarotongans the best cooks I'd encountered in the Pacific, but boy oh boy, those people might be a little bit better. The seafood they cooked in an umu was first-rate, and they also cook a large snail similar to our pūpū harakeke, and oh gosh, I'll never ever forget the taste of those things. Absolutely beautiful!'

Spending extended periods of time around the umu gave Hec the opportunity to ask his hosts about their own voyaging culture. Like many indigenous people across the Pacific, they confirmed that they had lost most of their customary knowledge. However, they were able to tell Hec that they had a long history of building and sailing large double-hulled canoes, and that several early European explorers had mentioned seeing fleets of canoes at the Isle of Pines. A number of drawings of Kunie canoes survive. One such drawing, sketched by trader Andrew Cheyne in 1841, depicts what Cheyne termed a 'war canoe.' It has a flat deck spanning twin hulls, and was powered by a single oceanic lateen sail. It's unclear just how far such waka ranged, but the size and construction of the waka in Cheyne's sketch suggest that they would have been well capable of inter-island sailing.

It wasn't a surprise for Hec that the Kunie had lost much of their voyaging lore by the 21st century, and he promised the local chiefs there and then that, should they be interested in reviving the art of navigation, he would always make room for any of their people at his wānanga. It was an offer Hec made wherever the opportunity arose. Like Mau and Nainoa before him, he clearly understood that a renaissance programme held in the hands of a few individuals was vulnerable. Nainoa Thompson discussed this issue in a *Mana* magazine article: 'There are some people who may want to bring people together but not all have the mana to do that ... but Hec's role in the Pacific is one of holding us together as a nation of peoples. We need to have a way to stay united in a collective way, Pacific-wise. For voyaging, as powerful as it's been in the '70s, '80s, and '90s, there is a risk of losing our navigation traditions if we don't transfer that knowledge ....'[2]

As the festival began to wind down, Hec's thoughts turned to the voyage home: 'We were pretty much ready to leave as soon as the festival finished, and for once the winds were in our favour, so after saying our farewells I was able to set a course directly for Norfolk Island. Even though the voyage was dogged by light winds, we enjoyed ourselves, especially when we had the opportunity to witness kūaka migrating south. There were thousands and thousands of them flying just above the surface of the ocean.' It was a mesmerising sight for the crew, many of whom had previously witnessed flocks of kūaka departing Aotearoa, and a reminder for Hec of nature's role in navigation. The land-nesting birds were flying on a precise course – a sure sign that land sat in the direction they were headed. In this case, that land was Aotearoa.

Four days after leaving Noumea, keen eyes picked out Norfolk Island cresting the horizon. Within hours, Hec had dropped Te Aurere's anchor 100 metres off Emily Bay, on the island's sheltered southern coast. Hec had briefly considered sailing through the gap in the reef and anchoring close to shore, but had ultimately discounted it as an option: the small passage through the reef made the inner bay a potential trap should they get caught by unfavourable winds.

The offshore anchorage proved suitable, and moreover, the shoreline had an interesting history dating back several hundred years. Hec: 'A few years before our visit they found evidence that Polynesians had lived there in the old days, so when they told me about it I said I would love to see where they had stayed and to mihi to the ancestors. I felt really bloody honoured too when I got to visit the site, especially as we had come to the island by waka.'

The site, among sand dunes, revealed the existence of a possible home and an adjacent paved marae-like area. Other finds in the vicinity had included shell and bone tools, basalt flakes, blades and adzes. Archaeologists also uncovered a considerable amount of obsidian sourced from Raoul Island in the Kermadecs, and a single piece of volcanic, glass-like rock that may have originated from New Zealand. It has since been determined that the settlement was occupied between the early thirteenth and early fifteenth centuries, but that people may not have lived there for the duration of that period.[3]

In part due to the wonderful hospitality the crew received, Hec delayed Te Aurere's departure several days, and she eventually left when strengthening winds promised the arrival of inclement weather. The decision to leave would prove opportune; by the time they had weighed anchor and started for home the threatening weather had begun to close in. Hec: 'We actually had a hell of a time sailing back from Norfolk Island. The weather wasn't cooperating, and we had a hard time making progress. Then, two days out from home, I woke up with a funny feeling deep down inside – the sort of warning you take seriously. It stayed with me all day long, and I was still wound up when the boys started yahooing after they spotted the North Cape later that afternoon. Well, I went off the bloody handle at them as soon as they started up. I told them that that wasn't the way to act, and if anything they should have been saying a prayer of thanks.' It was soon after that episode that an ominous-looking squall caught up with Te Aurere. As Anaru recalls, it came at them like 'a black wall. It was like a taniwha coming for us.'

While the normal course of action would have been to drop the sails and secure the boom, Hec didn't hesitate to order the crew to drop the entire rigging: 'Normally we just close the sails and ride it out, but this time I had the boys drop everything, and just as we got the rigging tied down, it hit us. We got thrown around for nearly an hour, and boy, I've never been in anything like it. At one point the canoe was picked up and thrown sideways like it was an empty matchbox.' It was a none-too-subtle reminder of the power of nature, and the group was somewhat subdued as they sailed into Doubtless Bay.

A few days later, as Hec relaxed at his Aurere property, he was able to reflect on the voyage. The crew had performed well and grown in confidence as the days at sea had passed, and Te Aurere had proven herself again. The only real frustration had been the canoe's inability to make port in Noumea. For a while after the voyage Hec toyed with the idea of installing a diesel engine in his canoe, but it never eventuated. Instead, he refocused his energies towards refining his waka taua-building skills. Indeed, the middle years of the decade were notable for the number of waka Hec built. Between 2005 and 2008 he oversaw the construction of seven full-sized waka, and completed a second voyaging canoe. Launched in late August 2008 to appropriate karakia and in the presence of the Māori King Te Arikinui Tūheitia Paki, Ngāhiraka Mai Tawhiti would double Hec's programme's sailing capacity, providing the means for additional crew to be trained. She would later sail in tandem with Te Aurere on the historic Waka Tapu voyage to Rapa-nui in 2012–13.

As the decade progressed, Hec continued his annual pilgrimage to Hawai'i for the International Festival of Canoes. While each festival presented its own particular challenges, 2002 was especially demanding. Soon after arriving at Kamehameha Iki Park, Hec and his team, including master assistants Eru Tepania and Hemi Eruera, discovered that they would have to draw on all of their experience to complete their waka. Hawaiian elder Ke'eaumoku Kapu explains what happened: 'We brought Hec a log about 6 feet [1.8 metres] in diameter, but when he cut it right down the centre, there was a beehive in it. That beehive never stopped him, though: he cut the log right in half and pulled a bit from someone else's log and spliced it on. We all watched him. We couldn't believe it. Nothing ever stops him, not even the bees of Hawai'i. Fittingly, the waka was named Ohanga Pī – the Bee House.' Among experienced waka-builders from across the Pacific, Hec was the standout craftsman of the festival. His skills were already widely acknowledged back home, but his ability to complete Ohanga Pī within the allotted time frame cemented his international reputation as a tohunga tārai waka – a master waka-builder.

Hec's work patching waka together wasn't restricted to canoes built in Hawai'i however. Back home, he assessed several waka that needed attention, including a historic waka taua housed at Ōtaua in Northland. In 2009, Hec arranged to meet with kaitiaki of the waka. He wanted their permission to carry out some restoration work on the hull. 'In 1940 there were two waka at Waitangi, and they were both named Ngātokimatawhaorua,' Hec explains. 'Tom Munu told me that there was a bit of a competition between the two groups, because the Ngāituteauru people from up in the north weren't happy that Waikato carvers were being brought up to build a waka in their own region, so they built their own to make the point.

'Unfortunately, their waka had been damaged after attending Waitangi all those years ago, and I don't think she had been in the water since. When I got the chance to have a good look at her, I quickly realised that I would need to virtually replace the entire bottom of the hull. When it was originally built they'd made the bottom of the hull a bit thin: it was only about 2 inches [5 centimetres] thick, so when I added to her I made the hull about 4 inches [10 centimetres] thick, which increased her strength and stability. There were some other parts of the waka that were rotten, too, so we had to cut a few sections out and put new pieces in.'

By the time Waitangi Day came around in 2010, word of the waka's relaunch had spread. Hundreds of spectators crowded the beach across from Te Tii Marae and along the nearby shoreline to witness the spectacle. Hec: 'It was a thrill to see her on the water again, especially when the two Ngātokimatawhaorua were paddled side by side. She was actually a very fast canoe, I think in part because the beam of the canoe – where it is widest – was positioned halfway along the hull. All the canoes I had been building up to that point had their beams two-thirds of the way back, so I picked up something new there. Now if I want a fast canoe I position the beam halfway back.' This is an acknowledgement typical of the man. With all his years in the game – with all his experience working on waka – Hec is still open to learning; still trying to perfect his art.

The relaunch of Ngātokimatawhaorua was the first of two memorable waka-related events for Hec during 2010. In October, he travelled to Europe to attend the handover of his waka taua Te Hono ki Aotearoa (The Link to New Zealand) to the Volkenkunde Museum in Leiden, Netherlands. The sixteen-man waka was the first of Hec's canoes to be based permanently outside of the Pacific. It had been commissioned for the museum by Toi Māori Aotearoa, the national organisation for Māori art and artists, and paid for by the Bank Giro Lottery in the Netherlands. In a unique arrangement, the waka remains the property of Toi Māori, but was loaned to the museum for 100 years. Robert Gable: 'Originally the Dutch wanted to buy a waka, but in the end it was decided that it was better to lend one to them, principally so we could begin a long-term relationship with them.'

Constructed by Hec and his assistant Hemi Eruera and finished by master carver Takirirangi Smith and his team, the waka was launched at Aurere on 26 June 2010, shipped to a Belgian port and then trucked to Leiden for the official handover. Its new home in Europe isn't the only reason it is a one-of-a-kind waka. Due to the nature of Te Hono ki Aotearoa's new home in the Netherlands, Hec was forced to make some changes to the standard design template. The waka was fitted with a shorter than usual taurapa to allow her to pass under Leiden's low bridges, and the hull was designed to turn on the proverbial dime, so she could be manoeuvred in the typically narrow canals.

There are some aspects of waka culture that are non-negotiable; one of the conditions of the loan of Te Hono ki Aotearoa was that the vessel's guardians in the Netherlands must learn the appropriate commands for the waka in te reo Māori. The Dutch were also obligated to reinforce their skills by sending a contingent of paddlers to Aotearoa each year to experience waka culture first-hand. While in the country, they would visit Hec's workshop in Doubtless Bay, before joining the crew of Ngātokimatawhaorua during the Waitangi Day celebrations. It's an arrangement that has been eagerly embraced, as Dutchman and waka kaihautū Koos Wabeke explained in an article in the *Northern Advocate* in 2011: 'The Maori culture has grabbed us pretty hard. They are trusting and give us a lot of responsibility, they are open and honest, they tell great stories and then listen to our stories. We are hooked on it. It's an absolutely amazing country, and this is one of the most beautiful experiences of my life.'[4]

In early 2011, Hec received an unexpected phone call from Karl Johnstone. Johnstone had consulted with Hec on a handful of exhibitions while working at Te Papa, and was now the director of Te Puia, the New Zealand Māori Arts and Crafts Institute in Rotorua. He was calling to ask whether Hec was interested in sailing his waka across the Pacific to Rapa-nui. In an earlier collaboration, Hec had starred in a short film to support Te Papa's *Voyagers* exhibition; in it, he had talked about his desire to close the fabled Polynesian triangle on Te Aurere. Now Johnstone was calling to offer him that very opportunity.

As Hec listened he began to realise just how serious Johnstone was, recognising the same resolve that he himself had shown some twenty years previously, when he had set out to build Te Aurere. Hec: 'That call changed everything. At one stage I was thinking I mightn't ever get the opportunity to sail to Rapa-nui, mainly because of the costs involved, so I was quite excited when Karl phoned. The 1995 voyage to Hawai'i was done on the smell of an oily rag, but this was going to be different. Basically all we had to do was provide the canoes and crew – Karl would look after the funding and PR side of things.'

Johnstone had identified a significant gap in the Institute's operations, one that Hec could help with. Johnstone explains: 'Sir Āpirana Ngata had a very clear idea for the purpose of the Institute when he started working on the legislation to set it up in 1926, and that was to protect, promote and perpetuate Māori arts, crafts and culture. At the time Ngata could see that Māori material culture was in decline, and he was particularly aware that wharenui, a pillar of Māori identity, were disappearing because the skills needed to build and maintain them were being lost. What's more, he understood that if we were to lose those pillars and the tikanga around them, then we as Māori would be lost.' Ngata's answer was to establish a Māori arts and crafts school, which opened in 1927.

'The reason I approached Hec was because in my view we have to fully understand the role of whakairo and wharenui to continue moving forward, and to do that we have to understand the arrival of waka. In fact I believe we have to understand the entire migration of our people, and importantly to understand our connection to the Pacific, because we can't appreciate the more recent developments in and around our material culture without knowing how we connect to the knowledge base, which is our Hawaiki kōrero.'

Johnstone's proposal included the establishment of a satellite Māori Arts and Crafts Institute school, to be named Te Wānanga-a-Kupe-mai-Tawhiti, at Aurere. It was a marvellous prospect, and one that would allow Hec to meet his obligation to pass on the knowledge that he had accumulated from Mau, Nainoa and others. The school's initial focus would be on carving, waka-building, sailing skills and navigation. Johnstone: 'There was already a definite alignment between Hec's programme and our values before we got involved. His kaupapa aspirations are about training people and continuing the legacy that he's created with support from people like John Rangihau, Simon Snowden and many others, and that's where we can add capacity and support. That is our focus, because what we are really interested in is making sure that what has been relearnt continues to be fine-tuned, continues to be developed, and continues to be passed on. That is what the Te Wānanga-a-Kupe-mai-Tawhiti carving school at Aurere is all about, capturing that knowledge and ensuring it is perpetuated into the future.'

One key aspect of the carving school has been a programme to transfer knowledge relating specifically to the construction of waka taua, largely funded by Creative New Zealand. Hec: 'It's a programme that allows us to pass on canoe-building skills to other groups, because that's one of the kaupapa that is still a bit shaky. A number of contemporary waka taua built outside of the north have been a little unstable on the water, so a large part of Hemi Eruera's role within Te Wānanga-a-Kupe-mai-Tawhiti is focused on passing on what we know about waka taua.'

While the plans for the land-based programmes were being made, Hec prepared for the voyage to Rapa-nui, which would represent a major test of crew depth and leadership. It would be the fifth major expedition for Te Aurere, and the first since Jack Thatcher had navigated her to Norfolk Island in 2007. It would also be the first voyage for Hec's second waka hourua, Ngāhiraka Mai Tawhiti; and the experience of Stanley Conrad, Jack Thatcher, Ray (Moko) Henare, Kiharoa Nuku and Mahara Nicholas would be needed to watch over and support the two crews, both of which featured some new faces.

As Johnstone explains, having crew members from as many tribes as they could reasonably accommodate was an intentional ploy: 'We realised that we needed to broaden out the knowledge associated with sailing and navigation, and to do that we needed wider iwi representation on the waka. That was one of the key outcomes for the voyage that Hec and I identified early on, and [because of the decision] we are now seeing a new hunger for engagement with waka. We also wanted to show that in the 21st century Māori can work collectively and break down some of those artificial borders that have become more hegemonic through the Treaty process, because those borders were never as impermeable as they have become today.' Ultimately, the two waka would carry representatives from ten tribes for the first leg of the voyage, to the Austral Islands. Additional tribes would be added to the register of iwi represented during the course of the expedition.

Although a significant investment of time and resources was undoubtedly required to train the new crew members, that expense was all part and parcel of growing the voyaging programme. The expedition was also an opportunity to promote several existing crew members into senior roles, including up-and-coming navigator Piripi Smith and three watch captains: Kiharoa Nuku, Mahara Nicholas and Brian Wiki. In addition, Haimona Brown, Ani Black, Emma Siope and Hemi Eruera cemented their positions as key individuals within the wider group: each were identified as potential leaders for the future.

The voyage was expected to cover in excess of 9000 nautical miles and would see the canoes departing Auckland in mid-August 2012, heading directly to Tubuai in the Austral Islands. There, the crews would rest before carrying on to the island of Mangareva in the Tuamotu group. In the final leg of the outward voyage, Te Aurere and Ngāhiraka would steadily make their way east to Rapa-nui, where Hec, by now in his early eighties, would meet them and recite a karakia shortly before they landed. After a layover at Rapa-nui, the canoes would loop back through the central Pacific, putting in at both Mo'orea and Rarotonga. They would then wait out the storm season at Rarotonga before embarking on the final leg home.

As befitting yet another winter voyage, rough weather was a constant during the first leg to Tubuai, and intermittent cloud cover provided a constant challenge for the expedition's principal navigator, Piripi Smith. Even so, when Hec joined his waka at Rapa-nui he was pleased to learn that the two crews had perfomed exceptionally under trying circumstances, and Smith had proven himself a more than capable navigator. Ngāhiraka Mai Tawhiti had performed well during her maiden voyage, as had the well-travelled Te Aurere. Twenty-one years after her maiden voyage, she was still a worthy flagship for Māori voyaging in the Pacific.

The voyage clearly lived up to Johnstone's expectations and promised to deliver long-term benefits, the significance of which he believed would continue to be realised in the years to come. In addition, the expedition also demonstrated the viability of traditional navigation, as well as strengthening relationships between Māori and many peoples of the Pacific.[5]

As Hec's standing throughout the Pacific grew over the first decade of the 21st century, his contributions to tribal affairs back home were also beginning to take on an amplified importance. With his voyaging years behind him, Hec began dedicating more energy to supporting the work of Te Rūnanga o Te Rarawa, Te Rarawa's governing council, which is charged with progressing the spiritual, cultural, social and economic growth of the tribe. Rūnanga chairman Haami Piripi explains Hec's role: 'The position Hec takes within the tribe is that of a senior elder statesman. He was born into a family with a history of performing public duties on behalf of the tribe, and he has emerged as a true leader. At the end of the day he is the judge of everything. If there is something that Te Rarawa is doing that he doesn't agree with, he is able to say no. There is no law or policy that gives him the right to do that, but the minute he voices concern over something, that's it. There is always a bit of room to wriggle, but he wouldn't normally say anything unless he was really definite, and when he is really definite, you don't question him. He has been a mainstay, along with Sir Graham Latimer, for all of our recent Treaty of Waitangi claims. He hasn't been an outspoken claimant, but he has been right there with us. We have presented numerous submissions to tribunals, and he has been fantastic because of the deep cultural context he is able to provide.'

Hec's influence is also evident in more mundane aspects of tribal life. One such example – the naming of classrooms for Te Kura Kaupapa Māori o Pukemiro, a school sitting on the outskirts of Kaitāia – highlights the depth of thought Hec expends on seemingly inconsequential tasks. Piripi again: 'The committee had been discussing appropriate names in the lead-up to the school's opening, but in the end Hector stepped in to overrule everybody's suggestions, and what we ended up with was absolutely fantastic: a set of tūpuna names to inspire our children.'

Hec says of the process: 'Some of the names being suggested at the time were just ordinary tūpuna – well, fair enough, they were ancestors, but they hadn't done anything particularly inspirational in their day. I suggested that we use the names of ancestors who had done things to prove themselves. Pātito was one tupuna who was chosen. He was famous for returning from the dead to try to straighten out his son Toakai, who was getting cocky because of the amount of mana he held. Pātito came back, challenged Toakai, and knocked him down a peg or two, so there was a lesson to be learned there. Tōhē was another. He had the mana to name many places in the Far North, including Te Oneroa-a-Tōhē [Ninety Mile Beach]. So the idea behind giving the rooms those names was that the kids could learn important lessons when they studied the names written outside their classrooms.'

Preparing upcoming generations for the future has remained very much to the forefront of Hec's thoughts in his later years, and his position as a kaumātua means that he has become a sought-after mentor. It is a role Hec takes seriously, but he expects those who seek his wisdom to be switched on when they approach him, as Haami Piripi explains: 'Hec is a very hard taskmaster, and he expects a lot from those who come to him; especially from the people closest to him. He has very, very high standards. It doesn't matter if it is digging a drain, backing a trailer or making a submission – whatever you do, you do it well, you do it properly, and you pay attention to the detail. If you approach him because you want to learn something, he won't teach you as such, but rather he will make sure that you can witness what you want to learn. In fact he'll often perform what you hope to learn there and then in front of you rather than teach you in a more formal way. So, for example, if you want to learn a karakia for opening a whare, he will recite it for you, and if you're good enough, you'll snatch it and put it in your kete. It can be tough, but people seeking to learn from him only succeed if they really want to.'

Perhaps due to his own limited schooling, Hec has taken a particular interest in the nature of formal education over the years: a fact that broadcaster Haare Williams can attest to first-hand. Williams first met Hec in the 1970s while he was travelling the country archiving the stories of kaumātua. He spent many hours in his company. 'Hec wasn't quite a kaumātua at that stage,' Williams recalls, 'but I realised that he was a fount of knowledge in relation to waka and the narratives that accompany them, so I started to interview him, and I needed to go back to Hec over and over again through the years.' Their discussions weren't always about waka; nor were they all recorded for the airwaves. Williams again: 'I remember sitting down with Hec and talking about how the education system could be geared towards an increased understanding of the Treaty in terms of the future of New Zealand. We were asking questions like: What did the Treaty mean in 1840? What does the Treaty mean now, and what is it going to mean in 200 years? His advice was good. He suggested targeting the education system at primary and secondary school levels. I think he was already advocating for the compulsory teaching of te reo in schools, but was very conscious of not isolating te reo from tikanga, from the Treaty, from the ethos of Māori philosophy. He saw that education was the key for the future of New Zealand: education that was tempered by Māori philosophies and by the Māori language.' Hec remains convinced that such an approach to education, tying in as it would the country's entire populace to the land and its history, is one with potential benefits for all New Zealanders.

Heke-nuku-mai-nga-iwi Busby is by any standard a living conduit to his ancestors. It is for this reason that he has been able to significantly assist in the renaissance of voyaging and traditional navigation. His influence in regards to waka culture is unmatched, certainly among his contemporaries, but he has remained reluctant to seek praise for any of his achievements.

It would be fair to say that there have been few men born in the 20th century who have had a more hands-on role in the revival of any aspect of Māori culture, and in the context of modern waka-builders Hec's contribution has been truly remarkable. Hec's interest in and influence on many matters impacting on the general well-being of Māori have seen him receive numerous national awards for services to Māori over the years, including being made a Member of the Order of the British Empire (MBE) in 1994, and an Officer of the New Zealand Order of Merit (ONZM) in 2014.

Karl Johnstone shares a few final thoughts, which echo those of many others interviewed by the author over the past decade for the purposes for this biography: 'You know, I think Hec's legacy is more than about carving or building waka or navigation. I think *heke nuku mai ngā iwi* is his legacy – his ability to bring together the people of the Pacific. I have travelled in the Pacific with him quite a lot, and overseas he is an incredible ambassador – albeit somewhat of a rough-cut diplomat. But he is considered a complete hero in many parts of the Pacific. If he didn't have that ability as an ambassador, we would be a lot poorer for it.'

It is indeed an exceptional man of any race who can hold influence in a sphere that reaches across an expanse the breadth of the Pacific Ocean – especially if that man is as humble as Hec Busby.

Heke-nuku-mai-nga-iwi Busby, son of Timoti Iehu and Winifred Ruth Busby and born in the family homestead on 1 August 1932, has not only succeeded in following in Tūmoana's wake; he has emerged as a worthy tribal leader in the mould of his more immediate ancestors Turuturu, Pōroa, Puhipi and Timoti Wharemate Puhipi. An inspirational and highly respected elder statesman and a tohunga in a number of schools of knowledge, including karakia tawhito, whakairo, mau rākau, kapa haka, hoe waka and tārai waka, he is a learned man with few living equals. Under the several names he is known by throughout the land and across the Moana-Nui-a-Kiwa – as Heke, Hec or Hector – he has fulfilled the prophecy announced when he was named, and his nation is the richer for it.

Notes

1 www.teaurere.org.nz/voyages_NewCaledonia.html, accessed 21 February 2014.

2 Maniapoto, M. 'The Bridge Builder of Oceania', *Mana* magazine, December/January 2006–2007, p. 19.

3 Anderson, A and P White.'The Prehistoric Archaeology of Norfolk Island, Southwest Pacific', in A Anderson and P White (eds), *Records of the Australian Museum*, Supplement 27 (2001), p. iv.

4 *Northern Advocate*, 7 February 2011, p. 13.

5 'Waka Welcomed Home from Epic Journey', http://www.stuff.co.nz/national/8689810/Waka-welcomed-home-from-epic-journey, accessed 1 October 2014.

AWARDS AND HONOURS

Throughout his lifetime, Hec has received the following awards and honours.

Ngā Tohu a Tā Kīngi Īhaka | Sir Kingi Ihaka Award
Awarded in 1985 in recognition of a contribution to strengthening the continuity of Māori culture through his support of ngā toi Māori.

New Zealand 1990 Commemoration Medal
Awarded to both Hec and Hilda individually in 1990 in recognition of services to New Zealand.

Member of the Most Excellent Order of the British Empire (MBE)
Awarded in 1994 for services to Māori.

Te Tohu Tiketike a Te Waka Toi/Te Waka Toi Exemplary Award
Awarded for 'outstanding leadership and services to Māori arts' in 1996, specifically in recognition of exemplary contribution to the development of ngā toi Māori.

Honorary Fellow, NorthTec

Bestowed in 2007 for 'outstanding and distinguished contributions to NorthTec, Northland and society'.

Northland Sailor of the Year

Awarded by Northland Regional Council in 2012, in recognition of achievements with waka in unifying the people of the north.

Te Tohu a Te Waka Toi

One of two special awards given by Creative New Zealand in 2013 (the other was awarded to Jack Thatcher) to recognise 'contributions to revitalising heritage Māori arts': particularly the revival of traditional Polynesian navigation and ocean voyaging using wayfinding techniques.

Officer of the New Zealand Order of Merit (ONZM)

Awarded in 2014 for services to Māori.

WAKA BUILT BY HEC BUSBY

The following is a list of waka built by Hec over his lifetime.

WAKA TAUA

Mataatua-Puhi
Te Ika a Māui (Mokopuna)
Te Au Kaha
Whakaangi
Hono-ki-Aotearoa

WAKA HOURUA

Te Aurere
Ngahiraka Mai Tawhiti

WAKA TĒTĒ

Hāwera
Rangi Marie
Ue Rangi
Whānau-Moana
Hine Moana

Pūnana Leo (built in Hawai'i)
Name unrecorded (built in Hawai'i)
Name unrecorded (built in Hawai'i)
Ohanga Pī (built in Hawai'i)
Tākitimu (built in Hawai'i)
Marriott (built in Hawai'i)
Rongo (built in Hawai'i)
Ohana (built in Hawai'i)
Tāne nui a Rangi (built in Hawai'i)
Te Pahū o te Rangi (built in Hawai'i)

WAKA TĪWAI

Tukariri

CREWS ON TE AURERE'S INTERNATIONAL VOYAGES

The following is a list of crew members on Te Aurere's international voyages between 1992 and 2013.

1992 VOYAGE TO RAROTONGA

AOTEAROA-RAROTONGA

Stanley Conrad, Jack Thatcher, Piripi Evans, Craig Subritzky, Te Aturangi Clamp, Paul Le Noel, Sam Hauwaho, Pakake Winiata, Mau Piailug (Satawal), Clay Bertelmann (Hawai'i), Max Yarawamai (Hawai'i)

On the support boat *Nam Sang*

Hec Busby, Martin Bercic, Willie More, Hector Morris Busby

RAROTONGA-AOTEAROA

Stanley Conrad, Jack Thatcher, Piripi Evans, Craig Subritzky, Te Aturangi Clamp, Martin Bercic, Willie More, Hector Morris Busby, Waingaroa (Magoo) Renata, Tai Mamaku

On the support boat *Nam Sang*
Cliff Harris

1995 VOYAGE TO THE MARQUESAS AND HAWAI'I

TAHITI-RA'IATEA
Hec Busby, Jack Thatcher, Martin Bercic, Tūrakuraku (Lux) Kereopa, Dean Waharoa, Hori Ahlers, Charlie Wilson, Robert Gable, Chris Irwin, Terissa Busby, Hiria Rutene, Pohe Luttenberger

RA'IATEA-TAHITI
Hec Busby, Hilda Busby, Jack Thatcher, Martin Bercic, Robert Gable, Tūrakuraku (Lux) Kereopa, Dean Waharoa, Hori Ahlers, Frank Waitai, Chris Irwin, Terissa Busby, Hiria Rutene, Pohe Luttenberger

TAHITI-MARQUESAS
Hec Busby, Stanley Conrad, Jack Thatcher, Piripi Evans, Martin Bercic, Tūrakuraku (Lux) Kereopa, Dean Waharoa, Hori Ahlers, Charlie Wilson, Chris Irwin, Paul Stanley, Frank Waitai, Heifara (Tahiti), Porutu (Tahiti), Carlos Hucke (Rapa-nui)

MARQUESAS-HAWAI'I
Stanley Conrad, Jack Thatcher, Piripi Evans, Martin Bercic, Tūrakuraku (Lux) Kereopa, Dean Waharoa, Hori Ahlers, Charlie Wilson, Chris Irwin, Frank Waitai, Heifara (Tahiti), Porutu (Tahiti), Carlos Hucke (Rapa-nui)

HAWAI'I-RAROTONGA

Hec Busby, Jack Thatcher, Tūrakuraku (Lux) Kereopa, Hori Murray, Carl Ahlers, Hori Ahlers, Te Taka Keegan, Carlos Hucke (Rapa-nui), Keahi Omai (Hawai'i), Sesario Sewralur (Satawal)

RAROTONGA-AOTEAROA

Hec Busby, Jack Thatcher, David Lewis, Hoturoa Kerr, Cliff Barton, Terissa Busby, Carl Ahlers, Robert Gable, Jenny Middlemiss, Tūrakuraku (Lux) Kereopa, Peter Rupapera, Hector Morris Busby

2000 VOYAGE TO NEW CALEDONIA

AOTEAROA-ISLE OF PINES, NEW CALEDONIA

Hector Busby, Piripi Evans, Deno Wahapu, David Nauer, Wiremu Tuhura, Anaru Reedy, Tomika Whiu, Ray (Moko) Henare, Lance Smith

ISLE OF PINES-NORFOLK ISLAND

Hector Busby, Piripi Evans, Deno Wahapu, David Nauer, Wiremu Tuhura, Anaru Reedy, Tomika Whiu, Ray (Moko) Henare, Lance Smith, Robert Gable, Robert Busby

NORFOLK ISLAND-AOTEAROA

Hector Busby, Deno Wahapu, David Nauer, Wiremu Tuhura, Anaru Reedy, Tomika Whiu, Ray (Moko) Henare, Lance Smith, Robert Busby, Wati Forbes

2007 VOYAGE TO NORFOLK ISLAND

AOTEAROA-NORFOLK ISLAND-AOTEAROA

Jack Thatcher, Anaru Reedy, Hemi Eruera, Wati Forbes, Emma Siope, Kiharoa Nuku, Waikarere Gregory, Sandra Schischka, Mahara Nicholas, Liam Ogden, Piripi Smith, Candice Reading

2012–13 VOYAGE TO RAPA-NUI

AOTEAROA-TUBUAI

Ngāhiraka Mai Tawhiti

Jack Thatcher, Mahara Nicholas, Piripi Smith, Regan Fairlie, Kushla Allen, Nathan Foote, Candice Paewai, Gerry Smith, Johnson Tumai-Totorewa, Ani Black

Te Aurere

Stanley Conrad, Kiharoa Nuku, Brian Wiki, Rahi Tamati, Hakopa de Beurs, Ray (Moko) Henare, Haimona Brown, Tahi Iwikau, Toiora Hawira, Te Miroa Mohi Maxwell

TUBUAI-MANGAREVA

Ngāhiraka Mai Tawhiti

Jack Thatcher, Mahara Nicholas, Emma Siope, Regan Fairlie, Gerry Smith, Kushla Allen, Candice Paewai, Johnson Tumai-Totorewa, Ani Black

Te Aurere

Stanley Conrad, Kiharoa Nuku, Brian Wiki, Ray (Moko) Henare, Hakopa De Beurs, Haimona Brown, Toiora Hawira, Rahi Tamati, Ta'aroa i Te Tapu (Tubuai)

MANGAREVA-RAPA-NUI

Ngāhiraka Mai Tawhiti

Jack Thatcher, Mahara Nicholas, Emma Siope, Gerry Smith, Kushla Allen, Candice Paewai, Johnson Tumai-Totorewa, Ani Black, Dr Wayne Ngata, Te Miroa Mohi Maxwell

Te Aurere

Stanley Conrad, Piripi Smith, Kiharoa Nuku, Ray (Moko) Henare, Haimona Brown, Martin Bercic, Hakopa De Beurs, Tahi Iwikau, Rahi Tamati, Toiora Hawira

RAPA-NUI–TAHITI

Ngāhiraka Mai Tawhiti

Jack Thatcher, Mahara Nicholas, Ani Black, Te Miroa Mohi Maxwell, Hakopa De Beurs, Kate Souness, Kahu Brown, Tamahau Tangitu, Johnson Tumai-Totorewa, Serafina Moulton Te Pano (Rapa-nui)

Te Aurere

Kiharoa Nuku, Ray (Moko) Henare, Toiora Hawira, Kuka Tukaokao, Parewhati Taikato, Emma Siope, Alfracinia Jacobs, Candice Paewai, Haimona Brown, Io (Kanko) Haoa Hotus (Rapa-nui)

MOOREA–RAROTONGA

Ngāhiraka Mai Tawhiti

Jack Thatcher, Haimona Brown, Mahara Nicholas, Tamahau Tangitu, TK (Genesis) Te Kuru, Rereao Carlson-Amiot (Tahiti/Moorea), Danny Asama (Hawai'i /Tahiti), Serafina Moulton Te Pano (Rapa-nui), Tauari'i Salmon (Tahiti), Taiau Tauira (Tahiti)

Te Aurere

Kiharoa Nuku, Toiora Hawira, Carlos Ahlers, Ray (Moko) Henare, Aden Ohlsen, Ani Black, Yves Heloury (Tahiti/Moorea), Tangaroa Murphy (Tahiti/Moorea), Willow Aubelle (Tahiti), Io (Kanko) Haoa Hotus (Rapa-nui)

RAROTONGA–AOTEAROA

Ngāhiraka Mai Tawhiti

Jack Thatcher, Haimona Brown, Regan Fairlie, Mahara Nicholas, Tamahau Tangitu, Awhina Twomey, Poihakena Dudley, Yves Heloury (Tahiti/Moorea), Taiau Tauira (Tahiti), Serafina Moulton Te Pano (Rapa-nui)

Te Aurere

Kiharoa Nuku, Toiora Hawira, Carlos Ahlers, TK (Genesis) Te Kuru, Ani Black, Ray (Moko) Henare, Aden Ohlsen, Terissa Busby, Hemi Eruera, Io (Kanko) Haoa Hotus (Rapa-nui)

GLOSSARY

Aotearoa	New Zealand
Atutahi	the star Canopus
haka	a ceremonial dance, often performed before a battle
hāngī	an earth oven
haumi	the join used to connect two sections of a waka's hull together
hui	a meeting
ihi	power, authority, essential force
iwi	a tribe
kai	to eat
kaihautū	the crew member assigned the role of calling the time for the paddlers
kaihoe	a paddler of a canoe
kaimoana	seafood

kāinga	a village
kaitiaki	a guardian
kapa haka	a Māori cultural group
karakia	a religious incantation, prayer
karakia tawhito	an ancient incantation, prayer
kaumātua	an elder
kaupapa	a cause or purpose
kei te pai	good
kete	a basket
kina	the common sea urchin
koha	a gift
kōhanga reo	a Māori language pre-school
kōrero	a talk
korowai	a cloak, covering
kūaka	the bar-tailed godwit
kuia	a female elder
kūkupa	New Zealand pigeon (Northern dialects)
kūmara	sweet potato
kura kaupapa	a Māori language primary, intermediate or secondary school
mana	authority, influence, charisma

mana whenua	territorial rights
manaakitanga	hospitality, kindness, generosity
marae	the open space in front of a meeting house
mātauranga	knowledge
mau rākau	fighting with Māori weapons
mauri	life force
mihi	to greet, pay tribute or acknowledge
muka	prepared flax fibre
nīkau	a native palm
pā	a fortified vilage
paepae	the orators' bench on a marae; the length of timber lashed along the join between the rauawa and hull on a waka
Pākehā	a New Zealander of European ancestry
pānui	a notice
paru	dirty
pōhara	poor
poupou	a carved ancestral post standing inside a building
pūhā	small leafy plants from the sowthistle family

puhoro design	the painted design on the hull, situated under the tauihu
rākau	the stick or baton placed on the ground during a wero, or ritual challenge to visitors
rangatira	a person of high rank
Rapa-nui	Easter Island
rauawa	topstrake or gunwale, attached to the sides of a canoe above the hull
raupō	bulrush
taha tangata	the human aspect of mankind
taha wairua	the spiritual aspect of mankind
Tai Tokerau	Northland
taiaha	a staff-like weapon used in hand-to-hand combat
Tāne	god of the forest
Tangaroa	god of the sea
tangata whenua	people of the land
tangi	a funeral
taniwha	a monster or water spirit living in a river, lake or sea
taonga	a highly prized object

tapu	under a religious or superstitious restriction
tauihu	the prow-piece of a waka
taurapa	the stern-piece of a waka
te reo	Māori language
tikanga	protocol
tī-tree	the cabbage tree
tohunga	an expert
tohunga tārai waka	an expert canoe builder
Tūmatauenga	god of war
tūpuna	ancestors
upoko	the head (in this case of a taiaha)
waiata	a song
waka	a canoe
waka hourua	a voyaging canoe
waka taua	a war canoe
waka tīwai	a dugout canoe
wānanga	an educational seminar or conference where traditional knowledge is taught
wero	a ritual challenge to visitors
whaikōrero	a formal speech

whakairo	carving
whakapapa	genealogy
whakatauākī	a quote
whakataukī	a proverb
whānau	family
whanaunga	a relative
whare	a house
wharenui	a meeting house
whenua	land, territory

INDEX

Bold type indicates photographs between the numbered pages.